Walking in the Vale of Clwyd
and the Denbigh Moors

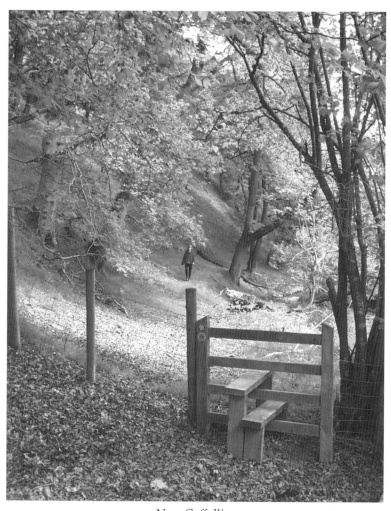

Near Cyffylliog

Walking in the
Vale of Clwyd
and the Denbigh Moors

by
Lorna Jenner

MARA BOOKS

First published in November 2000 by Mara Books,
22 Crosland Terrace, Helsby, Frodsham, Cheshire WA6 9LY.
www.marabooks.co.uk

All enquiries regarding sales telephone: 01928 723744

ISBN 1-902512-08-1

Cover photos:
Front: Field path near the village of Clocaenog (route 13).
Back: Ruthin and the Clwydian Range.

Text and photos on pages 50, 58, 72, 74 & 115 © Lorna Jenner 2000.
All photographs © Alan Roe 2000, unless otherwise stated.

Maps and photographs on pages 7,10, 20, 44, 86, 91 & 96 along with
cover photography © Carl Rogers 2000.

Wildlife sketches © Wendi Williams-Shiel.

British Library Cataloguing-in-publication data. A catalogue is available
for this book from the British Library.

Whilst every effort has been made to ensure that the information in
this book is correct, the author or the publisher can accept no
responsibility for errors, loss or injury however caused.

Maps based on out of copyright Ordnance Survey mapping

Printed and bound in Wales by MWL Print Group 01495 750033

Contents

Map of the area covered and location of each walk

Introduction

The Vale of Clwyd and the adjoining moorland of Hiraethog have much to offer the walker—varied scenery and wildlife, historic towns, picturesque villages and a rich history. They are often overlooked in favour of the more rugged Snowdonian mountains to the west or the long Clwydian ridge to the east but they are well worth further exploration. If you want to escape the crowds who climb Moel Famau or flood into Snowdonia each weekend, discover the unspoilt and relatively uncharted countryside that lies between them. This collection of walks will help you to explore these less well known areas. Each part has its own special character.

The central focus of the Vale of Clwyd is the valley itself, threaded by contrasting rivers, the Clwyd and its tributaries, the Elwy and Clywedog. Their characters are shaped by the rocks beneath. The Elwy and Clwydegog are fast flowing, particularly in the upper reaches, over rock and boulder clay

St Peter's church, Ruthin

Afon Clywedog, near Bontuchel

and their levels rise rapidly after heavy rain. The Clwyd is more sluggish as it runs over porous rock. Its levels are slower to rise after rain and it carries sand and silt rather than gravel.

Many of the walks have stretches of riverside walking but the contrasting characters of the rivers are best seen on the two walks that start from Rhewl. The Rhewl to Bontuchel walk follows the rocky Clywedog valley where the river tumbles over rocks between steep sided ravines whereas the Rhewl to Llanynys route is a flat riverside walk following the wide slower flowing Clwyd through cattle grazed meadows.

Viewed from the surrounding hills the Vale looks green and inviting. Lush meadows and pasture, edged with thick hedgerows, cover the wide valley floor. Sheep grazed fields, some divided by stone walls, dominate the lower slopes, interspersed with copses and areas of rolling parkland. Small farming hamlets, picturesque villages and historic market towns add to its special character. The spires and towers of churches stand out in the Vale and battlements of ancient castles and forts on the higher ground. Much of the land was owned by a few large estates and many of the grand country houses built by these wealthy landowners still remain. Several walks lead through or alongside the grounds of these houses, the most impressive being Nantclwyd Hall at Llanelidan.

The Hiraethog moors probably look much the same nowadays as they did 5,000 years ago when the warm, wet weather after the last Ice Age allowed grasses, mosses and heathers to establish themselves. Ever since Stone Age man hunted on the moors over 8,000 years ago, mankind has been harnessing the resources of the moorland. From the Bronze Age when farming techniques slowly developed, the moors have been used to graze livestock. By the 16th century cattle were regularly brought from the valley to the moors for summer grazing. The herdsmen lived on the moors with their stock, in simple one roomed stone shelters—hafods or hafotty—and some of these remain. In more recent times large areas have been flooded to form reservoirs, providing the only large stretches of open water in the area. The Aled reservoir was built first in 1906 and Llyn Brenig in 1976. The Brenig walk follows the dam wall and has fine views of the moorland.

Another more recent development is large scale forestry. Agricultural opportunities are limited on the moors due to the peaty acidic soils but conifers grow well here and many parts are now heavily forested. The Clocaenog walk explores part of the forest and the dark greens of the conifer plantations are an integral part of the landscape on many of the walks.

The lower level walks often have magnificent views of the surrounding mountains. Most of the walks in the eastern vale have wide views of the Clwydians, those in the west around Gwytherin and Llanfair Talhaiarn have spectacular views of Snowdonia but there are also panoramic views on the Mynydd-y-Gaer, Llanddulas Quarry and Clocaenog walks.

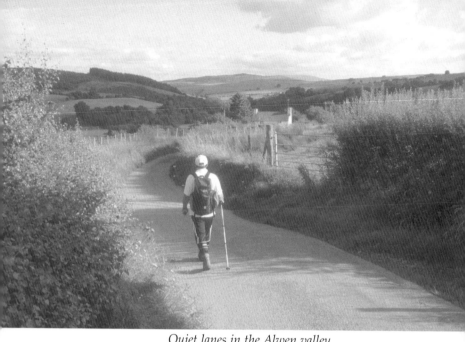

Quiet lanes in the Alwen valley

The routes use footpaths and bridleways wherever possible but some rights of way in the quieter areas are rarely walked and, as a result, can be difficult to follow, so there are also many sections on quiet lanes. These often make a pleasant addition to the walk as many are edged with thick old hedgerows and grassy banks dotted with wildflowers. The area is criss-crossed with old drovers' roads along which sheep and cattle were moved to market or between summer and winter grazing. Some are now shady sunken lanes, worn away by centuries of use, no longer used by stock and perfect for walking.

The unspoilt nature of the area is one of its greatest charms but there are often only limited facilities for the walker. Do not expect to find cosy teashops in the smaller villages that are far off the beaten track, and many of the characterful pubs only open in the evenings during the winter, so check before you set out or take flasks and provisions with you. The larger historic towns such as Denbigh and Ruthin, and many of the villages close to them, however, are well equipped for the visitor.

Most walks are enjoyable at all times of the year—the flush of spring flowers and newborn lambs; the meadows and moorland in summer, full of wildflowers and alive with birds and insects; rich autumnal colours and autumn mists in the valleys; the more open winter landscape with stunning views of snow covered mountains—all have their own qualities. A few of the walks, however, are best avoided at certain times of year. For example, the riverside south of Rhuddlan floods easily and should be avoided in wet weather and the moorland at Gwytherin can be extremely boggy and is difficult to navigate in the mist. The lower walks over farmland in the Vale can be unpleasant in damp conditions in June and July when the grass is long, before silage has been cut. Tastes and preferences vary and one person's idea of a gentle walk may be very different from anothers but I have tried to give advice in the introductory walk description.

History

The area has a long and chequered history. Some of the earliest human remains in Britain have been found here. Neanderthal Man used the caves in the limestone cliffs over 200,000 years ago, probably camping at the cave mouths and fashioning simple stone tools for hunting the mammoths and bison on the plains below. Gradually, over thousands of years, the nomadic lifestyle of these early hunter-gatherers was replaced by a more settled agricultural way of life. Communities further developed when metal working skills were gradually introduced from Europe around 2,400 BC. Stone Age cairns and Iron Age barrows, used for burial, are dotted on the Denbigh Moors and the limestone outcrops suggesting that, as the climate improved, the communities began to use the higher ground, as the flat valley bottom was too marshy. By the Iron Age some larger settlements had developed. The most obvious remains are of the defended hill forts—a series of ditches and banks—visible on hilltops throughout the area.

11

The ruins of Denbigh Castle

The Roman invasion included Wales but most of their military action was along the coast and the Conwy Valley. There were relatively few Roman settlements in the Vale or on the moors, although the Roman road linking the forts of Deva (Chester) and Segontium (Caernarfon) passed through the sites of Rhuallt and St Asaph, en-route to Tal-y-Cafn in the Conwy Valley.

After the Romans withdrew from Britain, the Saxons gradually took control of England but never succeeded in conquering Wales. They had a decisive victory against the Celts near Chester in 616 AD which effectively confined the Celts to the land that later became known as Wales, separating them from their kinsmen in Cornwall and northern England.

Conflict between the Saxons and the Welsh princes continued and for centuries the area was disputed borderland between England and Wales. In fact the old name for much of it, "Berfeddwlad", means "The Lands Between". One result of the constant warring was the building of Offa's Dyke, a long earthen ditch and bank, built by King Offa of Mercia (now the Midlands), to define and protect his border with Wales.

Skirmishes between the Welsh and Saxons continued despite the Dyke—the agricultural richness of the Vale making it particularly appealing to raiding parties. The Saxons won control of the northern crossing of the Afon Clwyd near Rhuddlan in 796 AD although King Offa was reputedly killed in battle here soon afterwards.

Following the Norman victory at Hastings in 1066, the Normans were quick to take control of England, but, like the Saxons before them, they were unable to extend their influence much beyond Offa's Dyke. They were however, not content to leave the Welsh unconquered in the mountains on their western border. William the Conqueror subdued potential uprisings by giving lands along this frontier to his most powerful barons who were free to plunder the Welsh kingdoms and extend their own influence. He thus solved two problems in one go. Once again the fertile Vale of Clwyd was an attractive prize to his northern Baron based at Chester.

The Normans erected a series of castles to consolidate their positions, but it was not until the reign of Edward I in the 13th century that Wales was finally conquered.

The Welsh prince Llywelyn refused to swear allegiance to the newly crowned Edward and, in retaliation, Edward invaded North Wales and forced Llywelyn to surrender. In the agreement that followed Llywelyn forfeited most of his lands leaving him with just the highlands of Snowdonia, whereas his unscrupulous brother Dafydd, who had fought on Edward's side, was rewarded with the lands between the Conwy and the Dee. However, peace did not last long as Dafydd soon resented the interference of English officials installed by Edward at Denbigh. The two brothers united in rebellion. They had some success at first taking the castles at Hawarden, Ruthin and Hope, but Edward's armies finally crushed them. Llywelyn was killed at Builth Wells in mid Wales leaving Dafydd to fight on alone but he was eventually caught and died a horrific traitor's death, being hung drawn and quartered at Shrewsbury. The heads of both brothers were displayed at the Tower of London and the Welsh were subdued for a period.

Edward rebuilt several Welsh fortresses in stone and commissioned others, developing a ring of castles in North Wales as a formidable show of strength—those at Rhuddlan and Denbigh are still imposing landmarks.

Peace was relatively short lived however and the area continued to be caught up in the struggles between the Welsh princes and the English rulers. The most powerful uprising was led by Owain Glyndwr, who declared himself 'Prince of

A double-naved church at Rhuddlan

Wales' in 1400 and began his rebellion by sacking Ruthin in retaliation for the seizing of some of his lands by its tyrannical English lord, Henry De Grey. Glyndwr enjoyed almost a decade of success in his struggle with the English crown but he eventually lost support and died in obscurity. He remains, however, one of Wales' greatest folk heros.

It was not until the late 15th century that the politics stabilized and peace and prosperity followed. It was during this period that many fine and lavishly endowed churches were built in the Vale of Clwyd. Many are double-naved and have beautifully carved wooden ceilings. The large churches at Denbigh and Ruthin are outstanding, but several of the smaller village churches have their own special charm. One of the finest is that at Llanrhaeadr, famed for its stained glass 'Jesse window' and that at Derwen with its intricately carved rood screen and medieval preaching cross in the churchyard.

But during the Civil War in the 17th century, the area was again at the forefront of action. Denbigh Castle was the last unconquered Royalist stronghold in Britain. Charles I took refuge there in 1643 after his defeat at Chester and there are many stories of skirmishes between Roundhead and Royalist troops in the surrounding area.

These stormy events have been much written about but the area's cultural richness should not be overlooked. Writers and artists were drawn here and it has long been a centre for Welsh culture.

Bishop Morgan, bishop of St Asaph from 1601-1604, played a vital part in giving Wales its own Bible and prayer book. Thomas Edwards, an 18th century playwright renowned as the 'Welsh Shakespeare', spent his later years in Denbigh. Beatrix Potter frequently stayed at her uncle's house, Gwaynynog Hall, near Denbigh and may have based her garden sketches for "Tales of the Flopsy Bunnies" here. Gerald Manley Hopkins, the Victorian poet who spent time at St Buenos college, Trechmeirion, wrote extensively of the beauty of the Vale of Clwyd. This is perhaps best illustrated by these lines from his sonnet "In the valley of the Elwy",

> *"Lovely the woods, waters, meadows, combes and vales,*
> *All the air things wear that build this world of Wales"*

Further west, Llanfair Talhaiarn was also a literary centre. John Jones, a 19th century poet who took the name "Talhaiarn" when he was made a bard at the 1836 Bala Eistedffordd, was born there. Many of his poems have been set to music and some are still sung today. The Harp pub where he lived became the favoured meeting place for local scholars and writers.

Llansannan with its monument to celebrate the five poets that lived there and Llangernyw with its Henry Jones museum, celebrating the life of this illustrious scholar, also have a cultural richness that complements the beauty of the surrounding countryside.

Farming

The Vale of Clwyd has long been renowned for the richness of its soil. Travellers told of a land where "throw in a stick and grass will cover it overnight". Agriculture remains the main land use and, to this day, the rich grass is still prized. Arable farming was also important until the 20th century and each settlement had its own corn mill. Farming practices have changed and transport networks improved so there is no longer a reliance on locally grown produce. Modern intensive arable farming is highly mechanised and needs large fields. Fortunately for the landscape of the Vale, the small irregularly shaped fields threaded by a network of narrow lanes are not ideal for this large scale production so the the attractive patchwork pattern of its landscape remains largely unaltered. Cattle still languidly graze on the lush riverside pasture and sheep dot the higher slopes much as they have done for centuries. Nevertheless the style of farming has undoubtedly changed.

Even grass production, to provide winter feed for the livestock, has intensified. Hay meadows, dotted with wildflowers, are less common nowadays as silage has taken over. Silage—fermented grass—is a nutritious winter feed for cattle and has become more popular as it is less weather dependent and of a more consistent quality than hay. After cutting hay needs turning in the fields for five days to dry out before baling. Silage however only needs to wilt for one day before being bagged for fermentation or, for larger scale production, chopped and packed into silage pits. Hence it is far better suited to the unreliable Welsh weather! Also, farmers can get several cuts of silage from each field between May and October which significantly increases production. Walkers during the summer months are bound to see the large round silage bales tightly wrapped in black polythene and silage pits, covered in polythene and weighted down with

Cattle grazing near Rhuddlan

tyres. The distinctive sharp sweet smell of silage around farmyards will become all too familiar.

Conditions on the moorland were too harsh for winter grazing but herdsmen took cattle onto the moors to feed on the new growth in the summer months. Sheep have gradually taken over as the main moorland grazing animal as they are hardy and need less attention than cattle. Dairy farmers nowadays tend to graze their cattle on the lower pasture during the summer, and overwinter them indoors, fed with silage.

Wildlife

The gently rolling farmland and open moors give the main character of the area but overall the landscape is a more varied patchwork. There are limestone outcrops, fast flowing streams running through steep wooded valleys, ancient woodland, conifer plantations, reservoirs and a flat wide estuary.

The flora and fauna are equally rich and diverse. Wildflowers thrive on the poorer soils in the limestone areas which, in turn, attract colourful butterflies. The pockets of wet woodland are luxuriant with huge ferns and mosses and the drier copses are dotted with primroses and violets in early spring and later carpeted with bluebells.

The moorland too is full of life. The purple heather covered hillsides in August, are broken up with patches of bright yellow gorse on the drier areas. There are wet flushes recognisable by the red and green spongy sphagnum mosses, dark green

Bluebell

Heather (ling)

18

rushes and the white seed heads of
bog cotton.

Birdwatchers too will find
plenty to see. On the open moors
red grouse may 'explode' from the
heather at your feet and you may be
lucky enough to glimpse black grouse in
clearings and at the edges of the conifer
forests. In the
summer the
p l a i n t i v e
haunting call
of the curlew
echoes across the
moors. They leave the coast in
the spring to breed on the moors.
Other summer visitors include
the sprightly little wheatear,
often seen perched on a
stone or clod of earth and
recognisable by its white
rump and black tail.

Curlew

Dipper

One of the most commonly seen and certainly the
most spectacular of the larger birds is the buzzard,
circling and wheeling overhead, with its distinctive
'mewing' call. Wading birds and wildfowl gather on
the estuary and reservoirs in the colder months;
herons are often seen flying slowly overhead or
standing in the shallow water looking for fish;
perky dippers bob across the streams; and
an assortment of tits, finches and other
small birds twitter and flit
between the
hedgerows.

Buzzard

19

Looking southeast from above Derwen

Acknowledgements

Many people helped me in the preparation of this book and it is their contribution that has turned the project from a long sometimes laborious job into a thoroughly enjoyable experience. Thanks to those who shared their expertise with me: - Phil Ebrell for his architectural comments, Malcolm Thomas for his farming advice and to Barbara Owsianka from Conwy County Borough Council Countryside Service and Adrian Walls of Denbighshire County Council for their advice on routes. Thanks also to the many people who accompanied me on walks and commented on the routes.

Special thanks to Alan Roe who researched most of the routes with me and introduced us to the world of digital photography. Also to Jack Rogers and David Telfer for checking routes. Finally thanks to publisher, Carl Rogers, for his help and encouragement through the long process of bringing the book from idea stage to publication.

Glossary of Welsh names

Afon .... *river*
Alt/Galt .... *hillside*
Bach .... *little*
Blaen .... *head of*
Bryn .... *hill, eminence*
Bwlch .... *gap, pass*
Bychan .... *little*
Cae .... *field, enclosure*
Caer/Gaer .... *fort*
Canol .... *centre*
Carreg .... *crag or stone*
Castell .... *castle*
Cefn .... *ridge*
Ceunant .... *ravine*
Clwyd .... *gate*
Coch/Goch .... *red*
Coed .... *wood*
Cors/Gors .... *bog or swamp*
Croes/Groes .... *cross*
Cwm .... *coombe*
Ddu/Du .... *black*
Dinas .... *city, fortress*
Dol/Ddol .... *meadow*
Dyffryn .... *valley*
Dwr .... *water*
Eglwys .... *church*
Fach/Bach .... *small*
FawrMawr .... *large*
Felin .... *mill*
Ffordd .... *road*
Ffynnon .... *well or fountain*
Foel/Moel .... *bare hill*
Ffridd .... *mountain pasture*
Garn .... *an eminence*
Glan .... *river bank*
Glas .... *blue-green*
Glyn .... *deep valley*

Gwern/Wern .... *alder coppice*
Gwyn/Wen .... *white*
Hafod .... *summer dwelling*
Hendre .... *winter dwelling*
Hen .... *old*
Isaf .... *lower*
Llan .... *church*
Llyn .... *lake*
Llys .... *hall or court*
Lon .... *lane*
Maen .... *stone*
Maes .... *field or meadow*
Mynydd .... *mountain*
Newydd .... *new*
Ogof .... *cave*
Pant .... *hollow*
Parc .... *park*
Pen .... *head or point*
Pentre .... *village*
Plas .... *house*
Pont/Bont .... *bridge*
Pwll .... *pool*
Rhaeadr .... *waterfall*
Rhos .... *moorland*
Rhiw .... *hill*
Rhyd .... *ford*
Tan .... *below, under*
Tomen .... *mound*
Traws .... *across*
Tref .... *town*
Twll .... *cavern*
Twr .... *tower*
Ty .... *house*
Tyddyn .... *farmstead*
Uchaf .... *upper*
Waun .... *moorland*
Y, Yr .... *the*
Yn .... *in*
Ynys .... *island*

Rhuddlan

Distance: *8 km/5 miles*

A fascinating walk exploring the historic parts of Rhuddlan and the meandering Afon Clwyd. The return route includes a stretch along a quiet road before following the old town ditch— a former Saxon boundary marker—to return to the town.

NB - Some of the riverside sections of this walk may become impassable in wet weather. The first section of the walk down to the river is the most interesting and would make an acceptable linear walk. Waterproof boots, or preferably wellies are recommended.

Start: *There is a small car park in Parliament Street just opposite the Community Hall or roadside parking near the castle. Grid ref: 024 782 (OS Explorer map 264).*

Rhuddlan is now little more than a bustling village. At first glance, it is hard to imagine its past importance to both the Welsh princes and their Norman conquerors, but this walk uncovers its more dramatic past.

Rhuddlan was always of strategic importance, situated on a hill overlooking the wide floodplain of Afon Clwyd. The first settlement grew up beside a ford which was the most northerly crossing point of the Clwyd—whoever controlled the crossing point controlled the easiest invasion route to and from the heartland of North Wales.

For five centuries it was a site of conflict and a natural point for fortification. It was the site of a great battle between King Offa of Mercia and the Welsh. Later a Saxon fortified borough and a Welsh princely palace were built here.

After the Norman conquest it became a Norman stronghold. Edward I rebuilt both the town and castle in the 13th century, making it his administrative centre for the area. He even wanted to build a new cathedral there to replace St Asaph.

The walk

1. From the car park turn right and walk down Parliament Street to High Street. Turn left along High Street and then take the first right into Church Street to detour to St Mary's church.

The church was built in the 13th century as part of Edward I's new town. It is a typical low double-naved Vale of Clwyd church with a simple sturdy tower set in a lovely churchyard on a promontory

above the river. The churchyard is packed with interesting tombstones and monuments—the 19th century Celtic cross to the Shipley family stands out and, at the back, a carved stone tribute to John Munt, a 19th century local sculptor.

Return to High Street and detour right across the river on the footbridge alongside the old stone road bridge for a good view of the castle.

You can see that the river is straight from the castle to the sea. Edward I had this stretch of river dredged and straightened to ensure it remained navigable to his large warships and supply ships. A new quay was built and it became an important port, still in use until two centuries ago when the railways gradually made it redundant.

Look out for cormorants flying up and down or swimming on the water and diving down for fish.

Walk back up High Street and, beside Church Street, cross over into Castle Street. In front of the castle where the road bears left, continue ahead on a minor road, Hylas Lane. Just beyond the castle, where the road bears left, take the footpath on the right alongside the castle grounds, signed to St Asaph and Twyt Hill.

In 1277 Edward I commissioned the building of a new stone castle nearer the town, replacing the original wooden one at Twyt Hill. It was to become a key member of his ring of castles in North Wales built as a show of strength against the newly conquered Welsh. It was the first to be built on a pattern of three concentric rings of fortification, an innermost diamond-plan stronghold, surrounded by an outer circuit of lower turreted walls, with a deep moat linked to Afon Clwyd.

It last saw action during the Civil War when it was held by the Royalists. They finally surrendered to Parliament in 1646 and the castle was slighted in 1648 to prevent further miliary use. The castle is now owned by CADW and open to the public from May - October.

At the end of the track go through a kissing gate and continue ahead towards the mound, Twyt Hill. Turn left at a

St Mary's church and the Celtic cross to the Shipley family

finger post on the path that skirts to the left of the hill—or you may wish to detour up Twyt Hill for superb panoramic views.

Twyt Hill is the site of the first Norman fortress, a motte—an earth mound, probably crowned by a wooden lookout tower—built on top of the natural hill with a wooden bailey beside it that housed the troops. It was built in 1073, at the command of William the Conqueror, to consolidate the Norman advances in the area. It passed between English and Welsh until Edward I recaptured it in 1277.

Continue on the clear path, walking above but parallel to the river. Follow the path as it bears left away from the river, near a caravan park, to a road. Turn right along the road, passing Abbey Farm on the left.

This is the site of the 13th century Dominican friary, built within the Norman town. Earlier monastic orders tended to live in isolation from the world but the Dominicans built friaries close to towns and their friars preached to the local populations. The numerous medieval preaching crosses in churchyards throughout the Vale of Clwyd reflect this practice. Little now remains of the friary but bits of the original stonework are incorporated into the farm buildings. From the road, in a niche in the barn, you can see an effigy that must have once been in the friary.

Continue along this lane until it divides into two tracks. Take the track that continues ahead into a field. Walk along the right-hand side of the field. You can see farm buildings ahead on the right. At the end of a second field, where a track bends right towards the farm, continue ahead to a stile in the hedge. Cross the stile and walk across the field to another stile in the bottom left-hand corner.

Look right across the field to picturesque Rhydyddauddwr Farm, an 18th century brick farmhouse with a central arched window and symmetrical sash windows on each side.

Rhuddlan Castle

2. At the bottom of the field climb a stile to a sunken grassy track. Turn left away from the farm and walk along a grassy track to a stile. Cross the stile into a field and continue along the right-hand field edge down to the river. Cross a ditch and walk with the hedge on your left, across a field with the meandering river on the right (NB - the path isn't clear, particularly when the grass is high in early summer). Continue ahead past where the field narrows and widens again, walking parallel to the left-hand fence, to an earth bridge over a ditch, where the river bends towards the field.

Many species of colourful damselflies and dragonflies can be seen near the water in the summer. Dragonflies are larger and sturdier with wings outstretched at rest, whereas damselflies are smaller and more delicate with wings held upwards and together at rest. The dark winged, magnetic greenish-blue bodied damselflies are particularly eye-catching and common.

Bear left across another field. After crossing another ditch (NB - ditch can sometimes fill with water and be difficult to cross), bear left and follow the fenceline partway along the edge of the next field to a stile.

The fields beside the river flood easily and there is standing water throughout the year which attracts shelduck, the occasional cormorant and flocks of waders in the winter.

You can see the squat tower of St Asaph cathedral ahead on the right. The cathedral has ancient origins. St Kentigern—a charismatic figure who later became patron saint of Glasgow—settled here in 560 AD with nearly 1,000 monks. When he returned to Scotland he consigned his Welsh monastery to his favourite pupil, a local man named Asaph. It is the smallest cathedral in England and Wales, and was destroyed time and again, situated as it was in the line of battle between the English and Welsh.

3. Cross the stile and walk uphill away from the river, along the right-hand field edge. Cross another stile in the top right-hand corner and continue across the next fields in the same direction. When a farm comes into view ahead follow a fairly clear track across a field to the farm. Walk through the farmyard and follow the path to the road. Turn left along the road and walk for approximately 2½km back towards Rhuddlan.

After 1km look for a mound on the left with a stone on top, just before a cluster of houses on the right. This is the base of a medieval preaching cross, perhaps used by the monks from the friary, when preaching to the local community.

4. At a T junction with the A5151, turn left and walk along the wide verge for a short distance. Turn left at the first junction onto Dyserth Road. Just before housing, turn left onto a signed path leading between a field and the backs of houses. Go through a small gate and continue along the path behind houses. Continue along this path which becomes enclosed by two old hedgerows (NB - can be overgrown and boggy) until you reach the end. Climb up the bank and over a stile out of the sunken path.

This sunken ditch, with a raised bank to the east, was part of the Saxon town defences. If you look back to the side of the ditch you can pick out the line of the old bank.

Turn right through a gate and follow the left-hand field edge to a road beside Abbey Farm. Cross the road and take the footpath, signed to Twyt Hill and Rhuddlan Castle, and retrace your steps back to Rhuddlan. Opposite the castle turn right and then left past a tea shop into the upper end of Parliament Street, passing some picturesque cottages and an interesting chapel on the left.

Denbigh

Distance: 6½ km/4 miles

The historic town of Denbigh with its ruined castle on the hilltop above the town, makes an ideal starting point for this walk. An exploration of the town, including an option to walk along the little visited medieval town walls, is followed by a peaceful walk through woodland at the base of the castle and along the picturesque Istrad valley.

NB - £5 deposit is required for the key to the walls. The key is available from the library (Telephone: 01745 816313 to check opening hours) and the castle custodian during the summer.

Start: *There is parking in a small public car park on Vale Street or a larger one by Safeways beyond Lenten Pool.*
Grid ref: 052 661 (OS Explorer map 264).

Denbigh's strategic hilltop position made it an obvious site for fortification during the turbulent Middle Ages—its name actually means 'little fortress'. Encircling the hilltop castle are the medieval walls, which were built for additional protection. The medieval town developed within the confines of the walls alongside the castle. Despite the castle's commanding position, the steep gradient and shortage of water restricted the development of a market centre, so a new settlement gradually developed at the base of the hill. By the 16th century the walled town had been largely abandoned and the earliest of the civic buildings in the lower town date from this period. The town became an important centre for the leather industry between 16th and 19th centuries. It specialised in the manufacture of gloves but also provided leather for the many shoemakers in the town.

The focal point of the High Street is the 16th century Old Town Hall which housed the market beneath the colonnades on the ground floor and the court and administrative rooms above. Now the town library and museum, it is the starting point for the walk.

The walk

1. From the Library walk up High Street.

The High Street and the roads leading off it are edged with many fine period buildings—look upwards at the rooftops and upper storeys to fully appreciate them as the lower shop fronts often do no justice to the buildings. Some have elegant Georgian facades which occasionally cover older half-timbered frames. For example, The Crown, overtly a grand Georgian coaching inn with plastered facade and tall windows, is heavily beamed inside, showing its older origins.

Crown Square opposite the library, where the present market is held, is worth a detour—the imposing stone building facing the square is the present Town Hall. It used to house a market and was later used as a fire station—the tall windows and doors were large enough for fire engines to enter!

Turn left up the narrow alleyway of Broomhill Lane, beside the 'Old Vaults' pub. At the top of the lane bear right past terraced public gardens, edged with groups of cottages, and climb up to Burgess Gate.

Burgess Gate gave access to the medieval town and castle. The local Welsh were not permitted to pass through the gate into the upper area and were forbidden to purchase land within the walls, so they lived outside the walls. (At the time of writing it was undergoing restoration but will soon be open to the public).

Walk through the gate and up St Hilary's Terrace to the green below the castle.

Ahead is the tower of St Hilary's church, all that now remains of the chapel built to serve the castle and medieval town.

Turn right and follow the road up to the castle. It is now managed by CADW and there is an entry charge to look round the interior, but you can wander freely around the outside.

This castle was once one of the strongest and largest in Wales. It was the chief stronghold of the Welsh Prince Dafydd ap Gruffydd until his defeat by Edward I in 1282. Edward commissioned the building of the stone castle, one of a chain of castles in North Wales that served to keep the defeated Welsh in check.

The commanding views from the green show what a formidable defensive position it occupied—it must have been almost impregnable!

The final military use for the castle was during the Civil War when Charles I sheltered there following a major defeat at Chester in 1646. Roundhead soldiers besieged the castle but the King had long escaped. The Royalists withstood the siege for 6 months but finally surrendered. The castle was dismantled in 1660 by the Roundheads and left to decay.

From the castle, walk back past St Hilary's tower and bear right along the lane leading down past the ruins of Lord Dudley's church below it.

Denbigh and its castle

Elizabeth I's favourite, Robert Dudley, held the lordship of Denbigh from 1563. A devout protestant, he began the church in 1578, intending it to replace the papist St Asaph cathedral as the centre of worship for the Vale. It was never finished—Dudley was very unpopular so money wasn't easily raised—but the lofty arches that remain give some idea of the scale and grandeur of his plans.

Just below Plas Castell, a group of Victorian Gothic buildings complete with battlements and tower, a small iron gate in the stone wall on the right gives access to the town walls. Detour to explore the walls if desired.

Following the ramparts above the town is a special experience from the moment you unlock the gate. Ferns and clumps of flowers grow between the stones, some sections are crumbling and the atmosphere is secluded and secretive. Firstly you are looking down to the gardens and rooftops of the town below. Further round there are wide views across the Vale, and you can imagine soldiers on sentry duty looking at a similar view many centuries ago.

Return to the gate and lock it. Turn right down road and, where the road bears left, take the footpath on the right below the walls. Walk downhill along the path for a few metres and at a path junction, take the narrower tarmac path on the right (do not continue downhill). Continue ahead on this path running parallel with the town walls and passing the grand buildings of Howell's School on the left. Continue walking on the same path that skirts through woodland below the walls, keeping the fence on your left.

The steep rock faces on the right gave good natural defences to the walls and castle above.

Continue on the woodland path, ignoring a path on the left just beyond school grounds, until you reach a road. Turn left along the road for about 100m, then bear right where the road forks, signed to Saron and Nantglyn.

The imposing building on the left is the North Wales Hospital, a Victorian mental hospital, built in grand Jacobean style.

2. Walk along the road for about 500m and where it bends right, take a signed footpath on the left, down a sandy track through woodland. Partway down the track turn right by a waymarker post onto a narrow stepped path. At a path T junction turn right onto a wider path that runs parallel to the river below and continue on this path. Just before a gate take a small path bearing left down the bank and over a stile into a field beside the river. Walk beside the river across the field. Continue on a grassy path through the next field passing a white cottage on the left. Cross a stile in the top left corner of the field, onto a road, beside a cottage drive.

Turn left along the road and after a few metres take a footpath signed on the right along the drive of a large house. (The drive is marked 'private' but it is a public footpath so walkers are entitled to use it. However, please respect the privacy of the owners as you walk through the grounds of their house!) Pass a vegetable plot on the right and the main house entrance on the left, then turn right alongside stables and go through large wooden gates onto a track. Turn left along the track and follow the path uphill. Continue along the path with trees on the right and the river on the left.

The grassy clearings are rich in spring and summer wildflowers— clumps of tall purple foxgloves line the woodland edge and the meadows are gold with buttercups.

Ignore a footbridge and waymarker on the left and continue ahead on the same path.

In the next field the small derelict and overgrown building on the right is the remains of Samuel Johnson's cottage. The 18th century writer who produced the first English dictionary, stayed here whilst visiting the Myddleton's of Gwaynynog. He was a renowned wit and moralist and is perhaps best known for some of his quotations such as, "It matters not how a man dies but how he lives" or "Marriage has many pains but celibacy has no pleasures."

At the end of this field where the path forks, turn right and walk diagonally uphill through woodland. Cross a stile into a field and follow the right-hand field edge with woodland on the right, climbing uphill to join a track. Bear right on this main track. Go through a gateway, ignoring a footpath and stile signed through the wood on the left, and continue following the track across a field to a gateway in the far right-hand corner. Go through another gateway and straight across a smaller field to a gate in a stone wall ahead, then continue a few metres ahead to a track leading from a farm on the left. Turn right through a gate and continue on the track, skirting the old brick walls of Gwaynynog on the right. Follow the track past the entrance to Gwaynynog gardens to the main drive.

Gwaynynog Hall was once owned by the powerful Myddleton family—Sir Thomas Myddleton became Lord Mayor of London and bought Chirk Castle in 1595. Brother Hugh owned the Welsh silver mines and pioneered the provision of London's water supply. A later owner was Fred Burton whose niece, Beatrix Potter also stayed there. Her garden sketches for "Tales of the Flopsy Bunnies" were based on the walled garden which is sometimes open to the public.

3. Cross the main drive, ignoring the entrances on the right to the house and associated buildings, and continue ahead on the track through a gateway with good views of the Clwydians ahead. Go through a gate at the end of the first large field and head diagonally-left to a gate in the far corner of the next field. Walk along the edge of the next field keeping a fence on the left. Cross another stile and continue downhill in the same direction with good views of Denbigh Castle on the left. Pass Galch Hill on the left.

This simple half-timbered house dates from the 16th century. It was owned by the Myddleton family and both Sir Thomas and brother Hugh were born there.

Climb a stile just past the house onto the lane. Turn right and walk down the lane for a few metres to another stile on the left into a field. Walk diagonally-right across the field. Cross a stone stile into the next field and continue ahead, keeping the fence on the right, to a stile in front of houses. Turn right along a path behind houses. At the end of the path turn left onto the road through housing. Turn right at the end of this road and left at a T junction soon after, following signs to the castle. Turn right again past Castle Lodge. Where the road forks, either detour right up to the castle again or bear left down to the Burgess Gate to descend back to High Street.

NB - Please don't forget to return key!

Henllan

Distance: *8 km/5 miles*

A pleasant walk centred on the attractive village of Henllan through rolling farmland and along old tracks.

NB - Some paths are prickly and overgrown in summer—shorts are not recommended!

Start: *There is limited roadside parking in the village near the Llindir Inn, Henllan.*
Grid ref: 024 681 (OS Explorer map 264).

Henllan lies at the heart of the fertile Vale of Clwyd and this rich farmland brought prosperity. The parish was much larger then— over 16 miles long and 7 miles wide. The grand houses dotted in the countryside around the village were owned by landed gentry families. They had considerable influence and their large estates provided employment for most of the locals.

The thatched Llindir Inn is one of the oldest buildings in the village, dating from 1229. Its name comes from 'llin', the Welsh word for flax, grown in the fields behind. It is the only remaining one of six pubs in the village that served the once large agricultural community and the quarrymen from the nearby limestone quarries.

The walk

1. Facing the Llindir Inn, turn right and walk along the road out of the village, signed to Llansannan (don't take left fork). After approximately 200m turn right onto a clearly marked footpath. Follow the path above the river through woodland. (You may need to detour around a tree stump but do not wander into the field).

Ferns and mosses thrive in the damp woodland of willow and alder.

Keep the river down on the left and follow the meandering path to the road.

Opposite is Henllan Mill, once driven by the fast flowing river, which ground corn from the surrounding farms, before most of the land was put to grass.

Turn right and follow the road uphill then sharply right back into the village beside the church.

St Sadwrn's church has very early origins and this is reflected in the village name—Henllan meaning 'old church' , from 'hen'—old and 'llan'—church. It originated from the cell of the 6th century hermit, St Sadwrn, but the present church dates from the 11th

century. Its most unusual feature is the separate bell tower perched on a rocky outcrop above the sloping churchyard. This was perhaps because the bells, summoning parishioners from the long parish to prayer, could be heard better from the hilltop than from the church below.

From the church continue along the road, signed to Trefnant, past the arch leading into playing fields. Take the first road on the right downhill, to rejoin the original road just above the Llindir Inn.

Turn left at the road junction and walk uphill, passing the Post Office on the right. Before you reach the school turn right up a lane, following a footpath sign and continue to a farm drive. Climb the stile to the left of the drive entrance and walk along the left-hand field edge alongside houses. Climb a stone stile ahead and follow a narrow woodland path (NB - May be quite overgrown!). Climb another stile and continue across the field with a fence and woodland on the right.

The Llindir Inn

The tall ivy clad ruin on the right is Foxhall Newydd—begun in the early 17th century, by the Recorder of Denbigh, who wanted to build the largest mansion in the district. It was never finished as he went bankrupt!

Continue ahead towards the farm buildings of Foxhall. Follow the path as it bears right over a stile and then left skirting the edge of Foxhall.

There are good views of the cluster of old stone buildings that make up Foxhall. The main house dates from medieval times but has been altered and added to many times.

Cross another stile and continue ahead across a field.

The raised banks in this field are actually the remains of an Iron Age enclosure which was probably occupied as a farmstead.

Don't follow the drive ahead alongside Denbigh Golf Course. Instead, bear right across the field to a narrow path, crossing the remains of an old stone wall that leads into the woodland. Go through a gate—waymarked here—and follow a narrow woodland track (NB - This path may get overgrown!) Go through another gate and continue ahead on a path bearing right away from the golf course. Cross the stile into a field, and a second stile 100m ahead, then walk diagonally-left across the field to the road.

There are now superb views of the Clwydian hills ahead.

2. When you reach the road turn sharp right by the side of a farm down a lane (not the road). After approximately 200m turn left over a stile (may be overgrown) onto a grassy track between two hedgerows.

This was obviously once a route of more importance—probably an old drovers' path that once linked farms and may have lead to Denbigh.

Keep going downhill on the same path crossing a stile (NB - lower section may be very muddy as cattle obviously use it). Pass Lodge Farm buildings on the left and bear left, following the waymarker, past the farmhouse, keeping the hedge on the left. Partway along the field cross a stile in the hedge onto the drive to the house. Turn right along the drive and walk to the main road.

There are good views of Denbigh to the left.

Turn right along the road (take care—busy road!) and walk along the verge for about 200m to a layby. Turn right onto a footpath signed from the layby and walk diagonally-left across the field to a stile in the middle of the hedgerow. Then walk diagonally-right for a short distance across the next field to a stile near the left-hand end of the fence. Cross a stile into a narrow field and turn left and cross a stile in the adjacent hedge into another field. Continue straight ahead, across the middle of the field, (route should be clear through crops). Cross two stiles over a small ditch into another field and bear left and follow the fenceline to a stile in the top left corner. Continue in the same direction keeping a hedge on the left. At the end of the field turn left over a cattle grid and then, at a track junction, turn right onto a surfaced track. Follow the track past cottages. When the track bears right into fields, continue ahead along a grassy path—a sunken lane between two hedgerows.

This old track must also have been an important drovers' route once as the river has a ford marked on the map.

Follow this path downhill—it may be very overgrown in places—to a stream. Ignore a path to the left and cross the stream on the right-hand side where the old ford must have been, to continue ahead on the same path. Ignore a second path signed to the left and continue on the path as it climbs uphill.

3. Turn right by a waymarker and climb steps and a stile out of the sunken lane into the field above. Walk along the fenceline for a short distance then, approximately halfway along the field, walk diagonally-left to a stile in the bottom left corner of the field. Cross a ditch at the next field edge, then turn right and walk diagonally across the field to a stile halfway along the fence at the bottom of the field.

Walk along the left edge of the next field towards Henllan— the church tower is a landmark on the hillside ahead. At the bottom of the field cross a footbridge over the stream.

The meadow beside the stream is full of plants that thrive in damp conditions—look for the spikey dark green rushes and the pink flower spikes of ragged robin.

Bear slightly left up the next field. When you can see Henllan church ahead again, aim for a hedge in the middle of the field and walk with the hedge on the right to a stile hidden in the top corner of the field to the right of a corrugated shed. Walk along the drive of a private house to join the lane that leads back to the road by the Llindir Inn.

The village of Henllan

41

Llanrhaeadr

Distance: *8 km/5 miles*

The pretty village of Llanrhaeadr is an excellent starting point for an exploration of the gentle rolling countryside that surrounds it. It is typical of the Vale of Clwyd—green, sheep grazed fields edged with mature hedgerows, pockets of woodland and streams in wooded valleys, all set against the backdrop of the dramatic Clwydian ridge to the east.

Start: *Some roadside parkingis available in the village. Start at the church.*
Grid ref: 082 634 (OS Explorer map 264).

Llanrhaeadr means 'church of the waterfall' and it is these two features that give the village its special character. The 'waterfall' in question is now little more than a stream tumbling down from a spring in the hillside above the church. Legend has it, however, that St Dyfnog lived here in the 6th century and did penance under the waterfall. His virtues reputedly gave the waters healing powers and pilgrims travelled miles to bathe in these holy waters.

St Dyfnog's church itself is the focal point of the village. Built from local limestone, embellished with mellow buff and red sandstone, it is a handsome double naved church with a sturdy tower. A delightful cluster of old stone buildings huddle around the church—the old smithy which is now a pottery; the carefully restored smithy cottage beside it; the whitewashed almshouses edging the churchyard, bequeathed for the 'relief of eight poor persons of the parish' by the lady of the manor in 1729; and the 16th century inn opposite.

The church is most famous for its stained glass Jesse window, which casts a soft light into the church, but there is also much more to admire. *Gently curving sandstone arches separate and support the twin naves with their magnificent 15th century wooden carved ceilings. The section above the sanctuary is particularly special, each panel is intricately carved with a different design and below are vine leaves and carved angel busts.*

During the Civil War Cromwell's soldiers kept watch for Royalists from the church tower during the siege of nearby Denbigh Castle. The soldiers were notorious for smashing windows with grave bones so the churchwardens dismantled the window and buried it in a dug out chest in the church grounds for safekeeping. It was later refitted and the huge chest that housed it now stands beneath the window.

The walk

1. After exploring the village and church, walk through the churchyard to the almshouses. Turn left through a small arch in the left-hand corner of churchyard. Cross the stream and turn right following a path uphill alongside the stream. Follow the path to a natural basin where the stream tumbles down the fern-clad hillside into the stone bath below. This is St Dyfnog's Well.

St Dyfnog's Well

It is incredible to find this carefully built deep stone bath, complete with steps in the midst of the woodland! Numerous slabs of dressed stone are dotted around the stream—remnants of the changing rooms and bathing areas built for the many visitors in its 17th and 18th century heyday.

From the well follow the path winding up the left-hand side of the hill. Go through a gap in the stone wall, turn right and walk along the path to a driveway. Turn left along the drive and then right into a field (clearly signed) opposite stone stables and a barn of the Vicarage. Diagonally cross the field to top left-hand corner. Cross a stile and follow the path to the road. Turn left and almost immediately right onto another waymarked path across the golf course. Cross the first fairway heading for a waymarker post straight ahead, beyond the green.

Carefully cross another fairway bearing left to a waymarker ahead, then walk along the fenceline with woodland on the right. Opposite buildings on the left, bear right along the fenceline, then climb over a stile into woodland on the right. Follow a narrow meandering path though woods to a track.

The woodland is carpeted with wildflowers in spring—bluebells, luxuriant spikes of early purple orchids and at the edges, masses of primroses.

Turn right along a broad forest track (left leads back to golf course). Take care to follow the yellow waymarkers through the wood as it is criss-crossed with tracks. Turn left at the next path junction along another woodland track, then turn right and follow the path to a stile at the woodland edge. Walk ahead across a field to a fence edging a small quarry. Continue walking, keeping the fenceline on the right, to a road.

2. Turn left along the road, then cross a stile into the second field on the right. Walk diagonally-left across the field to a stile in the far corner. Bear right in the next field, following the hedgerow towards buildings in the far right-hand corner. Cross a stile onto a track and then head right up the driveway of the next house, Ty Hen. Cross a stile on the right of the house into a field. Turn left and follow the field boundary alongside the garden, crossing the stile and continuing straight ahead along the fenceline. Cross another stile into the next field. Turn right and follow the hedgerow along the right-hand side of the next two fields. At the next field junction, cross a stile to the other side of the hedge. Turn left and continue in the same direction, gradually descending the hill. At the bottom cross a stile passing a small reservoir on the right (area may be boggy). Walk uphill along the field edge to the road.

Turn left onto the road and follow it downhill for approx 500m to a small crossroads. Continue straight across onto a quiet lane. When it becomes wooded on both sides, take the left-hand fork just before the main lane bends to the right. Follow this lane, running parallel to the river below, to buildings around Llewsog Hall. In front of the first house bear right following a track past farm buildings. Turn right, over a small bridge to another lane. Turn left and follow the winding lane for approx 1.½km.

The huge conifers dotted in first field on the right indicate that this was once parkland associated with Llewsog Hall—the grand white Georgian mansion glimpsed through the trees on the left.

There are good views across the valley and Moel Famau soon becomes visible ahead. You may see lots of pheasants in the fields and along the lanes.

3. Ignore forestry tracks crossing the lane and continue uphill a short way to a signed footpath on the left. Follow the path down an old sunken lane with tall hedgerows on either side. At the bottom cross a stream and follow the path uphill bearing right on the opposite side.

Charcoal burning was in progress by the stream at time of writing—look for the round metal charcoal pets in which the charcoal is made and stacks of wood.

Continue up the hillside on a small meandering path. At the top edge of woodland cross a stile and continue along an old track (NB - may be boggy). Go through a gate onto the road. Turn right along the road and continue for approx 1km.

Continue down the lane past Pen-y-Bryn on the left with the golf course on both sides. At a road junction turn left along a minor road with Bryn Morfydd Hotel down on the right. Turn right onto the footpath used earlier to return to the village. Cross the field and turn left onto the drive of The Vicarage. Walk to the road and turn right. After a short distance turn right onto a path running parallel to the road, beside an old brick wall. Continue to the end of the path, bringing you out by the almshouses above the churchyard.

Rhewl to Llanynys

Distance: *7 km/4½ miles*

A flat, gentle circuit along two rivers with superb views of the Clwydian hills. This circuit could be added to the contrasting Bontuchel route to make a long figure of eight walk—the Drover's Arms would be a good place to stop for lunch.

NB - An easy flat walk but some of the stiles are not easy to negotiate and the ground may be boggy in wet weather.

Start: *Park in Rhewl on the wider streets or in a car park by the recreation ground.*
Grid ref: 110 604 (OS Explorer map 264).

The walk

1. Walk back to the main road and turn right towards Denbigh. Just before the stone road bridge turn right onto a waymarked footpath into a field. Walk diagonally-left across the field to the river.

Cross a stile and follow a grassy path behind gardens, keeping the river on the left. Follow this path just above the river through several fields, passing a small pond and the grounds of an attractive old house on the right. Cross a stile on the left in the hedgerow, walking towards the river bank, and after 20m cross a second stile on the right and walk along the hedgerow parallel to the river.

Continue beside the river ignoring a wooden footbridge on the left. (Some of the stiles are rickety or difficult to spot).

Herons, with their long wings and distinctive slow wingbeats, are common. You may also hear the plaintive 'coor-li' call of curlews.

When you reach a larger stone footbridge turn right and walk along a track leading from the bridge heading towards the Clwydian hills.

There are now wide views of the hills. Moel Famau, the highest point of the Clywdian Range stands out, crowned by the remains of its jubilee tower which was built to commemorate 50 years of George III's reign. The original tall column blew down in a fierce storm just 52 years later. Its base was renovated in 1970 and, in 1977, was once more used to commemorate a royal jubilee when it was the site of one of the chain of beacons lit to celebrate Queen Elizabeth's silver jubilee.

Follow the track along the field edge to a gateway in the right-hand corner of a field, at a junction of three small streams. Walk through a gateway over one stream and go straight across the next field to a gate at the far side. Cross the next small field, heading for a gate in the far left corner and cross onto a track.

Turn right on the track and left onto the road. Walk along the road into Llanynys.

The views are magnificent now. Can you pick out the ramparts of the Celtic hillfort on Moel Arthur, to the left of Moel Famau?

2. Walk past the church and pub and turn right onto a path signed beside the pub.

Llanynys—'church of the island'—sits on flat land between the rivers Clwyd and Clywedog. Looking at the church bell tower standing out above the flat fields, it is easy to imagine that it may once have been on an island above the surrounding marshes. The parish church of St Saeran was once very influential, the site of a 6th century monastery and the mother church of southern Dyffryn Clwyd. Llanynys is now a quiet hamlet clustered around the simple stone church and its ancient churchyard with gnarled yews and tabletop tombs.

Inside the church is large and spacious, befitting its former importance. Opposite the entrance is a large medieval wall painting of St Christopher carrying the young Jesus across a river—the patron saint of travellers was often painted opposite church doorways so wayfarers could easily glimpse his image and be preserved from 'fainting or falling' all that day.

Walk down the path beside the pub past a row of cottages on the left. Cross a stile into the field. Cross the field diagonally to the right until opposite the church, then continue straight ahead past two large trees in the middle of the field to a bridge and stile in the opposite hedgerow. Cross the bridge over a ditch and a stile. Then bear right diagonally across the field

Bellcote, Llanynys church

to the hedgerow and follow the field boundary round as it curves left to a stile in the corner, beside a pink painted house.

Cross the stile and walk through a small enclosure planted with trees. Over another stile and walk along the left-hand edge of the next field. Cross a stile onto a track where a drive joins from the left.

Cross the bridge over the river, then climb right over the wooden slatted part of a fence and immediately left over another section. Turn right again to walk along the field edge with the river on the right below.

You're walking parallel to the Clwydians now so the views are superb once again.

Continue along the riverside through fields, crossing wooden lathe fence stiles. Cross the road and continue along beside the river, keeping it on the right and the Clwydians to the left.

50

Dippers—small brown birds with white bibs—are commonly seen on the river, bobbing on stones or flying rapidly down the river. They walk underwater to feed on river insects, tadpoles and worms.

Climb a ladder stile into the field. Pass the grand crenellated buildings of Clwyd Hall school on the left. Cross a stile into the next field, below a farm, cross the field and continue along the riverside passing farm buildings on the opposite bank.

There is a magnificent black poplar in the middle of the field, recognisable by its twisted bark and attractive in spring with its red tinged buds. The rounded hump of Foel Fenlli is behind it, crowned by a large hillfort.

3. At the next bridge turn right on the road to cross the bridge and then left onto a footpath. Continue walking along the opposite bank.

Ahead are good views to Ruthin church and castle.

Pass a footbridge crossing the river then turn right along the hedgerow just past it, to a farm (Plas-y-Ward). Walk through the farmyard, past whitewashed farm buildings and bear right passing a barn with stone arches on the right. Walk along the farm drive to the road.

Turn right along the lane and left at a T junction. Turn right just past playing fields to return to the village.

Black poplar with the Clwydian Range behind

Rhewl to Bontuchel

Distance: *7 km/4½ miles*

This walk leads across fields and along the steep wooded hillside above Afon Clywedog, then returns along the rocky riverside into Rhewl. It is idyllic in late spring with bluebells and freshly opening leaves or in the dappled shade of summer. It is special too in the colder months when the river is in spate.

Start: *Park in the car park by the recreation ground in Rhewl or on the roadside in the village centre.*
Grid ref: 110 604 (OS Explorer map 264).

The walk

1. From the Drover's Arms pub turn right and walk along the main road over the old stone bridge. Cross the road just after the bridge opposite a small cottage. Take the clearly signed path along a metalled farm drive beside a cottage.

Continue uphill along the farm track through woodland. Ignore the woodland tracks on either side until you reach a clear fork in the main track which is signed with yellow footpath waymarkers. Take the right fork and cross into a field. Continue walking along the right-hand field edge beside woodland.

At the far end of the field turn left in front of a barn and follow the fenceline to a stile in the hedgerow ahead. Continue ahead, gradually climbing uphill through fields, keeping the fenceline on your right and following the waymarkers towards woodland ahead.

On the right you pass a large pond which attracts wildfowl. There are superb views back to the Clwydians with mixed woodland clothing the valley sides.

Cross a stile into woodland and continue ahead, bearing slightly left, walking through tall conifer woodland along a clearly waymarked path.

The woodland floor is almost bare of vegetation here due to the lack of light penetrating through the foliage of the closely packed conifers—only occasional mosses and ferns where a pocket of light strays through. Compare this with the mass of greenery under the broadleaved trees further on—particularly rich in spring before the full tree canopy is out with bluebells, white stitchwort, and clusters of violets and primroses.

Continue along the woodland path into more open mixed woodland, that skirts fields on the right and woodland on the left.

Continue straight ahead at a footpath junction, keeping the field edge to the right.

Cross a stile into fields and continue straight ahead, with woodland in the valley on the left and farm buildings on the right. Cross a stile at the end of the field, back onto a narrow woodland path that skirts along the top of a steeply wooded valley, with fields to the right.

It is superb here in spring looking down the hillside when the wild cherry is in blossom with the dark greens of the conifers and paler greens of the freshly opening leaves of the deciduous trees. On the right before the path junction there is a dense carpet of bluebells beneath beech trees—a deep blue haze against the grey beech trunks.

2. Bear left down some steps to a path junction (turn right if you wish to detour down to Bontuchel village which has a pub for refreshments). Turn left and follow the woodland path for approximately 500m as it gradually descends to the river. Continue beside the river all the way back to Rhewl (approximately 3km).

After about 500m pass a footbridge on the right which gives access to the riverside on opposite bank—a good spot for picnics.

In spring the smell of the white flowered wild garlic that tumbles down the river banks is almost overpowering. The river bed is much rockier than the slower flowing Afon Clwyd and it is edged by rocky outcrops and crags. Look for unusual rock formations in the river bed—can you spot the giant stone 'turtle' in the river just before a kissing gate? The rock isn't porous so water levels can rise quickly and, in the winter months, the river is a fast flowing torrent.

The Bagot family had a large estate—over 17,500 acres—here in the 18th and 19th century. This path is known as 'Lady Bagot's Drive', as it was a favourite of hers and was once a scenic carriage route up to the Bagot's mansion at Pool Park.

Continue along the riverside path to a kissing gate. Go through the kissing gate and follow the track that leads between two cottages. Continue on the track as it bears right back to the riverside and continue walking along the riverside path.

You may notice a straight smaller stream running alongside the river and some old stonework chanelling it under the path—this may be a leat that drew off water to provide power in the past.

Continue straight ahead along the track, past the farm buildings of Rhyd-y-Cilgwyn farm, and bear right over the stone bridge.

Amongst the modern barns and outbuildings are several much older timber framed buildings. The farm and Rhyd-y-Cilgwyn house itself, further along the river, were also part of Lord Bagot's estate.

Continue to the main road and cross to return to Rhewl.

Looking towards the Clwydians

Ruthin

Distance: *10 km/6½ miles*

An exploration of this historic town and a pleasant circuit along the river and across farmland to picturesque Llanfair Dyffryn Clwyd. The walk back to the town is across fields and lanes with superb views of the Clwydian Range.

NB - It can be very wet walking across the fields in June before the silage has been cut!

Start: *There is plenty of parking in the car parks near the Craft Centre.*
Grid ref: 125 585 (OS Explorer map 264).

Ruthin has had a turbulent history—its name means 'red fortress', referring to its hilltop castle. In the Middle Ages the area was much disputed borderland between England and Wales. The Welsh and English inhabitants mixed little. The Welsh lived in Well (Welsh) Street and Mwrog Lane, whereas the English kept close to the castle for the protection it gave in Castle Street and Dog Lane.

The town saw conflict on several occasions, most dramatically when it was sacked by Owain Glyndwr in 1400, in his revolt against the tyrannical English Lord Grey of Ruthin. Most of the buildings were burned down and the town was completely rebuilt in the early 15th century. Many of these half-timbered medieval buildings still remain.

The walk

1. From the roundabout by the Craft Centre, walk up Market Street to St Peter's Square in the centre of the town.

The imposing stone building on the left towards the top of Market Street is the Town Hall and adjacent is the Market Hall which still houses regular markets. The livestock market is now held on the outskirts of the town.

Narrow winding streets, lined with tightly packed old buildings of assorted styles and materials, climb steeply up the hillside to St Peter's Square. The square itself is edged with a wonderful mix of buildings—half-timbered, brick, whitewashed and stone. Look upwards at the rooftops—wavy and uneven with old mellow tiles and slates and an array of windows. The elegant Georgian Castle Hotel dominates and, beside it, the Myddleton Arms with its three tiers of dormer windows, known as the 'eyes of Ruthin'.

One of oldest buildings, built in 1401, is now the National Westminster bank. It used to house the Old Courthouse and had a gibbet where criminals were hanged on the north west wall!

This route through the town takes in some of the most attractive streets. (Alternatively, you may prefer to just wander at will around the town centre before picking up the walk by 'The Wine Vaults' on the corner of Castle Street and St Peter's Square.)

Walk to the Post Office at the opposite end of the square from the Nat West bank, behind which you can see the tall spire of St Peter's church. Enter the churchyard through tall wrought iron gates on the right of the Post Office.

St Peter's church, Ruthin

This large church was founded in 14th century as a 'collegiate' church, staffed by a community of priests, who lived in the Old Cloisters which adjoin it. It stands out from other Vale of Clwyd churches as it is the only one with a spire, added during a Victorian restoration, which is a landmark for miles around (You can tell the spire is more recent as the stone is much more regularly sized and shaped.)

An attractive cluster of buildings edge the churchyard—the lofty cloisters with their pointed windows, the simple single storey almshouses and, at the back, the original grammar school buildings.

Return to the square and walk along the right-hand side. Take the first right down Clwyd Street which is packed with period houses and shops.

Many of the buildings are medieval timber framed but were refronted during the 18th and 19th centuries. Towards the bottom, opposite the Star Inn is the Town Gaol. The building edging Clwyd Street dates from 1775 when relatively few prisoners were held for long periods. The taller imposing Victorian building at the back was based on Pentonville and looks more secure and austere, complete with its small barred cell windows.

Walk back up the opposite side of Clwyd Street and bear right where the road forks up a narrow lane, Upper Clwyd Street, passing the 15th century Spread Eagle Bookshop on the right.

At the junction with St Peter's Square turn right down Castle Street, with the colonnaded Wine Vaults on corner.

Castle Street too is packed with period houses. Most notable is the half-timbered Nantclwyd house on the right, one of the oldest townhouses in North Wales.

Ahead is the gatehouse to Ruthin Castle. The castle was begun in 1277 as part of Edward I's formidable ring of castles built as a show of strength after his capture of North Wales. It saw much action during the subsequent Welsh revolts but was last used for military purposes during the Civil War when it was a Royalist stronghold.

The Roundheads laid waste to the castle after the Royalist defeat in 1646. The present house was built within the confines of the medieval castle in 1826 in Victorian Gothic style and was for many years a grand private house, whose owners entertained fashionable Victorian and Edwardian Society. It is now run as an hotel.

Just before the castle gatehouse, turn right under an arch and follow a narrow path between stone walls, known as Cunning Green. Follow the path through a second arch. Then bear left and follow a paved path alongside the castle walls.

There are super views of the gaol, watchtower and rooftops of Ruthin from here.

At the end of the path turn right and then immediately left. Then turn left again through a gate into Cae Ddol, the playing fields. Continue ahead, keeping the castle walls on your left and the river on the right—you may hear the calls of the castle peacocks!! Pass through a small kissing gate and continue alongside the fence until you reach a stone bridge across the river.

The river is clean and full of life. Small white flowers of water crowfoot float on the surface during the early summer and you may see dippers—small brown birds with white bibs, bobbing up and down on rocks in the river. The bridge is a good viewing place.

2. Go through the small tunnel under the bridge, then turn left and walk along the left-hand side of the field to the road. Cross the road and turn right to walk along the pavement beside the road for about 800m, ignoring a lane on the left. Just before a road on the right, take the signed footpath on the left through a gate. Walk diagonally-right across the field to a footbridge in the far left corner. Cross a stile onto a farm drive and turn left over a footbridge. Follow the drive to a farm.

Just before the farmyard go through a gate into a field on the left, then turn right and walk parallel to the barn across the field to a gate in the hedgerow ahead, just to the left of a

Church of St Cynfarch and St Mary, Llanfair Dyffryn Clwyd

large willow. Go through the gate and walk across the next field to a gate in the opposite fenceline. Beyond a gate follow a track uphill towards farm buildings, passing a raised bank and pond on the left.

The raised bank is the remains of a moated medieval homestead which was presumably replaced by Ffynnogion farm, the farmhouse ahead on the left, which dates from the 16th century.

Where the path bears left to farm buildings, keep walking straight ahead with the hedge on the right, to a stile in the corner of the field. Go straight across a small field and cross a stile into the next field. Continue across the next field to a stile beside a water trough, then walk diagonally-left across the next field to a ladder stile beside a large white house. Cross a very narrow field to the road. Turn right along the road and then left almost immediately through a small kissing gate onto a footpath along the left-hand field edge. Keep going in the same direction across two fields to the road. Turn right and walk along the road into Llanfair Dyffryn Clwyd.

The village centre is particularly attractive with its stone almshouses, village school and White Horse pub set around the fine 15th century church. There are superb views of the southern Clwydians from the back of the churchyard.

3. Turn left into the churchyard and then, after exploring, leave through a small lychgate beside the churchwarden's house. Walk along the lane to the road and turn left along the road. Follow this road for just over 1km. Where the road bears sharply right turn left onto a farm track (signed footpath) beside a lodge house. Continue along the track, passing Plas Newydd farm on the left.

17th century Plas Newydd is just visible through the trees in its grounds on the left. The row of limes edging the track and the dotted parkland trees in the surrounding fields suggest that its formal grounds once extended further. There are superb views of the Clwydians along this section of the route.

At the end of the track turn left onto the road and after 250m, take a signed footpath on the right, beside the drive to 'Merllyn'. Walk along the right-hand field edge. Just after a gate and field junction on the right, cross a stile in the hedgerow and then walk along the right-hand side of that field, now walking towards the Clwydians.

Continue to the end of the field, then cross a stile in the hedgerow just beyond. Continue walking towards the Clwydians along the next field edge. Cross another stile and walk across the middle of the field, parallel to the left-hand hedge, to a gate in the hedge opposite (walking towards Moel Famau now), then continue along the left-hand edge of fields to the road.

Turn right along the road and left at a T junction, signed 'Llanbedr'. Opposite the lodge of Bathafarn Hall, turn left onto a lane leading past Llanrhydd church.

It's hard to imagine that this simple little church was the mother church of the Welsh settlement that became Ruthin. The present building dates from the 15th century and there is the shaft of a medieval preaching cross in the churchyard.

4. Take the footpath signed on the right about 200m past the church, then walk alongside the left-hand fence to the first gate. Go through this gate (waymarked) and continue ahead keeping the hedge on the right and ignoring a stile on the right at the field boundary. Cross a stile into the next field and continue in the same direction along the edge of the field and across another small field to the road. Cross the road and turn left to walk along the pavement (NB - Take care, busy road!). Pass Bryn Hyfryd School on the left and the grand buildings of Ruthin School on the right.

The Grammar School that was originally in the churchyard of Ruthin church was moved to these grand purpose-built buildings in 1891. When prisoners escaped from the town gaol, boys from Ruthin School were occasionally used to help run them down!

Turn right along the main drive to Ruthin School. Beyond the school bear left and walk downhill along a private road edged with houses. At the end of the road cross Greenfield Road and walk to the roundabout by the Craft Centre to complete the walk

The Clwydians from Llanfair Dyffryn Clwyd

Llanelidan

Distance: *8 km/5 miles*

A delightful circuit from this picturesque village through parkland and across wooded hills.

NB - Some sections through the woodland may be quite overgrown in summer and can be muddy—trousers and boots are recommended!

Start: *Park on the road in Llanelidan or by the village hall. Grid ref: 109 505 (OS Explorer map 264).*

Lanelidan's 15th century church with its pretty double bellcote, village hall, handsome stone pub and cricket green form an attractive group, standing amidst fields, whilst the main housing is on a nearby lane.

The walk

1. From the village hall turn left and walk along the road passing the pub and church. Just after the road crosses a stream, turn right onto a footpath alongside the stream. Walk past the cricket pavilion gradually bearing left away from the stream across the field to a stile in a wooden fence. Cross a stile and continue to another smaller stream—aiming for the stag headed oak. Cross the stream on a large stone slab to the right of the oak, then turn right and climb diagonally up the field to a footpath waymarker and a stile onto the road. Turn right and walk along road for approx 400m to an attractive cluster of old farm buildings on the right. Don't turn into the driveway but cross a stile on the left of the drive entrance, following a waymarked footpath into a field, keeping the farmhouse on the right.

Cross the field, heading towards a clump of pines on a hillock. Walk to the left of the hillock then downhill towards a lake, making for a stile in the far right-hand corner of the field by weeping willows at the far end of the lake. Cross onto the road.

The lake and the surrounding wetland attract waterfowl, particularly in winter—black and white tufted duck and Canada geese are common.

The grand country house ahead is Nantclwyd Hall. The gardens have been elaborately restored including stone gazebos, ornamental bridges and sculptures. (A short detour right along the lane gives views of the gardens and there is a small castellated water tower beside the lake on the right.)

2. Turn left and walk along the lane past the Hall to the main road.

You pass a gateway on the right flanked by huge stone pillars crowned with stone eagles.

Turn right onto the main road and walk along a broad

Ornamental bridge by Nantclwyd Hall

grassy verge for approx 400m. Just beyond a stone bridge on the right, turn right onto a footpath that crosses the course of an old road into the woodland. Walk through the woodland for about 60m on a narrow path that leads onto the cropped lawns of Nantclwyd Hall. Walk with the river on the right, crossing the drive to the house and continue ahead to a gate in the fence.

There are superb views of the brick mansion as you look down the driveway. The oldest part dates from the 17th century but it was extended and altered in the 18th and 19th centuries. In the 1950s and 60s it was elaborately remodelled by Sir Clough Williams-Ellis, the architect famous for the design of Porthmeirion.

Climb a stile beside the gate and walk along the riverside to a pretty wooden footbridge. Cross the footbridge and walk diagonally-left across grassland.

There are more good views of the mansion with the lake in front. Colourful dragonflies and more slender bodied damselflies dart across the edges or rest in the vegetation at the lake edge in the summer.

Continue to a gate in an electric fence and cross, then climb diagonally-left uphill across parkland. Walk through dotted trees between a large fenced copse on the left and the main woodland on the hilltop to the right.

Continue contouring along the hillside parallel to the wood on the right. Pass a second smaller fenced copse on the left. At the far corner of the copse turn right and walk to a gate and stile leading into the woodland.

Follow a narrow path leading left uphill through the trees.

The strong smell of wild garlic, with its dark green leaves and white flowers, fills the woodland in early spring, and is followed by a carpet of bluebells in May.

At the top of the wood go through a gate and bear right onto a track along the field edge for about 80m. Go through a gate into the next field and then turn left at a waymarker and walk across the field to another wood—there is no longer a fence across the field but two large boundary trees roughly show the way. There are two gates into the woodland—you take the one on the right!

There are good views of the Clwydians on the right as you walk across the field.

Walk along a path (may be quite overgrown in summer) which bears left through the woodland. Continue on the path to the woodland edge beside two derelict cottages. Cross a stile in the fence, to the right of the second cottage, beside a corrugated barn, then walk straight ahead for a few metres along a rutted muddy path. At a path junction (may be muddy and difficult to see paths clearly) bear right on a path which runs alongside a stone wall with woodland on the right. Continue downhill to a gate and stile with a cottage on the left. Cross the stile and bear right along a track.

Walk along the track for 500m towards the road. Cut off a corner by crossing a stile into a field on the right before the road and walk diagonally-left across the field to a stile leading onto the road. Walk along the road for a few metres then, just before the drive to a house on the right, cross a stile on the left into a field and walk along the field edge, with woodland on the right.

Partway down the field cross a stile on the right into woodland and follow a meandering path across the woodland for about 150m to a stile leading into a field on the far side. Continue ahead following the left-hand field edge, keeping woodland on the left. Cross another stile and continue ahead, now with the fenceline on the right.

Continue straight ahead across the field keeping fairly close to the fence and woodland on the left. Cross a stile in the corner of the next fence and then turn left immediately over another stile into woodland and follow the path to the right, continuing in the same direction as before along the woodland edge. The path is difficult to find in places and may get overgrown in summer.

Wildflowers flourish on this grassy limestone bank at the woodland edge. In spring cowslips abound; look also for the spikes of early purple orchids.

Climb away from the fenceline to skirt along the top of a small rocky outcrop above the field, contouring the hillside, keeping the fenceline on the right below. At the corner of the field bear left through thinning woodland and then bear right to find a stile on the right leading back into the field. Turn left and walk ahead with thinning woodland on the left. Continue in the same direction, going through an old gateway. Continue across the next field with the hedgerow on the right to the road.

Turn right onto the lane and then at a T junction turn left and walk along the lane until you come to a pretty stone

Nantclwyd Hall

chapel on the left. Just opposite the cottage attached to the chapel turn right and cross a stile into the field. Then bear left across the field down to a stile in the hedgerow below. Turn right and walk down the road for 1km back to Llanelidan.

Llysfaen & Llanddulas Quarry

Distance: *5 km/3 miles*

A refreshing walk, climbing the limestone hill above Llysfaen, walking through pasture and leafy woodland on the lower slopes with dramatic cliffs and panoramic sea views from the hilltop.

NB - The section leading up to the quarry is steep.

Start: *Park in the lower part of Llysfaen, beside the bus stop, toilets and playground, at the junction of Tan-y-Craig Road and Dolwen Road.*

Grid ref: 893 767 (OS Outdoor Leisure & Explorer map 264).

The walk

1. Walk past the playground and turn left up Dolwen Road, passing a chapel on the right and then bearing right along the road. 100m beyond the chapel, turn right along a drive in front of houses, signed "North Wales Path" (NWP). Continue along this drive and a few metres past the drive to 'Bryn Celyn' on the left, turn left over a stile into a field, signed "North Wales Path". Walk across the top of grassy fields, with a stone wall on the left, contouring along the hillside.

To the right are wide views of the rolling Vale of Clwyd—a farmed patchwork landscape with irregularly shaped fields, edged with thick hedgerows and pockets of woodland.

At the end of the wall, ignore a stile onto a track on the left and continue ahead, walking parallel to the track. Pass a caravan site on the left behind a stone wall. Pass a stile and waymarker, and bear slightly left, still contouring round the hillside, following the direction of the waymarker. Pass a breezeblock building on the left, then turn left down the side of the building and right on a grassy path beside rubble. (This section is a bit difficult to follow but keep looking for waymarkers and skirt around a caravan park.) Continue contouring along the hillside, with a fence on the left, crossing another field boundary with a stile and waymarker.

Continue in the same direction until you reach a stile in the fence on the left. Cross a stile and turn right onto a track that still contours around the hillside. Where the path bears right, continue ahead, over a ladder stile into a field. Continue straight ahead along a grassy track. Where the track dips, a

Looking out to sea from the limestone cliffs below Llanddulas Quarry

few metres ahead, walk diagonally-left to a waymarker just visible on the hillside to the right of a stone wall on the left (the path may not be very clear in summer). Pass the waymarker and continue uphill passing the end of a stone wall on the left. Cross another stile and bear right across a field along a narrow path.

Wildflowers thrive on the poor thin soils above the limestone bedrock. Wild thyme, with its pink flowers and small scented leaves, delicate blue harebells, and ladies bedstraw, a small creeping plant with clusters of tiny yellow flowers, are all common in the summer. There are also patches of more acidic soil on which purple flowered bell heather and bracken flourish.

The variety of flowers provide food and shelter for many insects. You may notice the papery cocoons of the burnet moth in the summer. This distinctive red and black moth is one of the few day flying moths and is frequently seen on the rough grassland around the quarry. A variety of colourful butterflies thrive also—delicate blues, browns and coppery oranges—and, if you look carefully, you may also see grasshoppers camouflaged in the grass.

Cross a ladder stile over a stone wall and follow the waymarker straight ahead across grassland. (NB - It may not be very clear in summer when the bracken and grass are high.) Do not go left along the path that leads up to a high limestone crag. Find another NWP waymarker just below the crag and continue ahead on a narrow path through bracken that skirts along the base of the crag.

Follow the path for approximately 500m to a gate. Go through the gate and continue along the path down the hillside, heading towards the coast. The path leads through woodland, with occasional rocky outcrops. Ignore a footpath crossroads and continue on the same path until you come to a T junction of paths. Turn sharp left here, leaving the North Wales Path which is signed right down to the road below.

2. Follow this broad track as it gradually winds up hill. At a path T junction, just below the quarry fence, turn left and follow a narrow track. Walk along the path for approximately 1km, with the fenced-off quarry above on the right (you cannot see much but you can often hear it!) and woodland on the left, gradually climbing to the top of the hill. After a very steep section, go through a kissing gate and onto the hilltop.

There are superb panoramic views from the hilltop: the coast with the Great Orme protruding out to sea to the west, with the working quarry in the foreground; Snowdonia to the southwest; Llanddulas and the sea to the north; wooded hills edge the valley to the east with the Clwydians on the skyline in the distance and the lush Vale of Clwyd unfolds to the south. The line of rubble that was once a rampart on Pen-y-cordynn-mawr hillfort on hillside to the east is clearly visible.

From the top, walk back to the quarry fence and follow it around the quarry to the west. (Alternatively you can walk along the left-hand side of the hill to the path that leads back down to the ladder stile and retrace your steps back to the village.) Turn left alongside the first hedgerow, walking away from the quarry (may be overgrown and prickly in summer!). Climb the ladder stile in the bottom right-hand corner of the field onto a grassy path, between two fields. Follow this track as it bears left and then runs between two stone walls, until you reach a farmyard.

Go through a gate and walk past farm buildings along the farm drive to the road. Turn right along the road and continue for approximately 750m to a T junction, opposite a pretty chapel, attached to Holly Cottage. Turn left and descend the hill back to Llysfaen.

Mynydd-y-Gaer (route 10)

Mynydd-y-Gaer & Llanefydd

Distance: *8 km/5 miles*

A refreshing walk over Mynydd-y-Gaer—site of an Iron Age hillfort— through woodland in the valley and then contouring around the base of the hill back to Llanefydd.

NB - There are some steep sections up Mynydd-y-Gaer.

Start: *Park in the public car park in the middle of Llanefydd beside the church and village hall and on the opposite side of the road to the Hawk and Buckle Inn.*
Grid ref: 982 706 (OS Explorer map 264).

Llanefydd is a sleepy little village set amongst gently rolling farmland. Its focal point is the fine double-naved church with the whitewashed old inn opposite.

The walk

1. From the car park turn left and walk along the lane out of the village, towards Llanfair Talhaiarn, passing the school on the right. Opposite a lane joining from the left, go through a gate into a field on the right. Walk along the left-hand edge of the field. In the top left corner, with Plas Heaton farm ahead, go through a gate and turn left to walk along the left-hand field edge to the next hedge, heading towards Mynydd-y-Gaer. Go through a gate, partway along the hedge, then continue uphill along the left-hand edge of the next field. Climb a high stile in the top left corner and continue uphill

75

across a small field, over a stile into a
small enclosure and through a gate onto
the road by Ochor-y-gaer.

Turn left and walk down the road until it bends sharply
left. Turn sharp right along a lane with a 'no through road'
sign. Turn left onto a grassy track immediately past Bron
Hwylfa cottage. Follow the track uphill, bearing slightly right
at a path fork onto a narrow grassy path. Go through a small
gate onto the open gorse-covered hillside. Follow a narrow
grassy path through the gorse, bearing left along the hillside.

*The top of Mynydd-y-Gaer is wide and open, with panoramic
views—Snowdonia to the west; rolling pasture and tree-clad hills
with small reservoirs in the foreground to the south; the Clwydians
to the east and the sea to the north. The ditch and bank which still, in
part, surrounds the summit, are the remains of an Iron Age hillfort.*

The commanding views and steep sided slopes must have made it an ideal defensive site.

In summer the gorse is full of activity—the small birds flitting around with dark backs and paler orangish underparts may be whinchats and stonechats. Their habitat gives the whinchat its name as 'whin' is an old name for gorse. Listen for a sound like two pebbles being banged together which is the distinctive call of the stonechat.

When you can see a fence on the right and reservoirs below on the left, turn right on a narrow grassy path through the gorse to reach the top of Mynydd-y-Gaer where a modern cairn, in the field to the right of the path, marks the highest point. (Alternatively you can continue on the other path that contours round the summit following the ditch and raised bank of the hill fort. This is not an official right of way but is clearly defined and rejoins other path just above 'Ty-newydd'.)

Leave the top via a grassy path leading over to the northern side, between two fences. Descend the hill, joining a track

Afon Elwy west of Mynydd-y-Gaer

coming from the right by a cattle grid, and continue downhill, passing Ty-newydd on left.

Where the track splits, take the less clearly defined path to the right, walking with gorse and grass on the left and an old stone wall on the right. Follow the grassy path towards a farm. Then turn left in front of the farm wall and walk downhill beside the wall. Where the main path turns right at the corner of the wall, continue ahead onto a very narrow path that bears right through the gorse. Follow this track as it zigzags down the hillside through the bracken to the lane below.

2. Turn right on the lane and go through a gate. A few metres after, turn left down a farm drive (Tan-y-Gaer). Just before the farm turn sharp right down an old track between two hedges. At the bottom of the track where it enters a field, turn right along another track.

Follow this track for over 500m as it gradually descends the hillside (NB - can be very muddy). At the bottom of the hill go through a gate into a field and turn left across the field to a small gate in the far left corner, leading into woodland. Walk along the woodland path with the river on the right. (NB - the path is narrow and uneven in places.)

Follow the woodland path to a footbridge on the right. Cross the footbridge and walk across a field towards a white house. Turn left into grassy woodland just before the gate of the driveway. Then walk parallel to the river along a very narrow grassy path that may be overgrown with nettles and thistles in summer. Near a fence on the right continue in the same direction, keeping the fence on the righthand side, for approximately 400m to a gate. Beyond the gate, take the clear path diagonally-right uphill to the edge of the field, then cross a second field to a gate in the opposite hedge. Go through the gate and walk uphill to another gate in the top left corner of the field. Follow the left-hand fenceline and, at the top of the field, cross a stile on the left into woodland and then turn immediately right onto the road.

Plas-uchaf Reservoir

Turn left and walk downhill for about 500m and soon after passing the drive of Dolganed farm on the left, turn left onto a small lane. At the next road junction turn left again and follow this lane for 1km, over the river (Afon Elwy) and past a caravan park, then steeply uphill and sharp left into a hollow and uphill again to a gate. Go through the gate and turn right onto a grassy path that contours round the base of Mynydd-y-Gaer.

Follow this peaceful track, passing a small reservoir on the right. Beyond the reservoir, go through a small gate and continue ahead, ignoring the path to the left, through woodland. When this path reaches a road junction (lane leading up Mynydd-y-Gaer is ahead), turn right and walk downhill along the lane to another junction. Turn left and, where this lane meets a more major road, turn left again and walk along this road for approximately 1km back into Llanefydd.

Llanfair Talhaiarn

Distance: *8 km/5 miles*

A refreshing walk from picturesque Llanfair Talhaiarn, leading along the peaceful Nant Barrog valley, then contouring around Moel Unben with superb views of the Snowdonian peaks, returning to the village along a peaceful lane.

Start: *There is plenty of parking in a car park beside the bridge leading into the village from the A548.*
Grid ref: 927 702 (OS Explorer map 264).

The walk

1. From the car park exit beside the toilets, turn right along the main road into the village, past the Black Lion pub, into the square. Walk through the square. Just past the Post Office turn right along a tarmac path, leading uphill. After a few metres the path forks but continue ahead uphill to a road beside the church.

The church, set on the hillside in a particularly pretty churchyard, is well worth a visit. The monuments inside demonstrate how much village life was dominated by one family, the Wynnes, who owned nearby Garthewin Hall from the 17th century. The most lavish are those of the family themselves but some of the simpler tablets on the north side of the church are in memory of valued servants. In the churchyard there are gravestones erected for a gamekeeper and another for the Garthewin coachman.

To the right of the church drive, under the old yew tree is a granite obelisk which marks the grave of John Jones, a local 19th century poet who was made a bard at the 1836 Bala Eistedffordd and took the

80

name 'Talhaiarn' after that. Many of his poems have been set to music and some are still sung today. He was born in the adjacent house, Hafod Y Gan, which was then 'The Harp Inn', and became a meeting place for scholars and poets.

A few metres further along the road is the village school with its unusual octagonal bell turret.

Turn right past the church, then immediately left onto a lane running steeply uphill. Follow this lane out of the village, passing the drive to Nant Isaf Farm on the left. About 100m further up, just beyond farm buildings on the right, turn left into a field at a gateway with white wooden boards beside (no waymarker).

Follow the hedgerow along the left-hand side of the field, with Nant Isaf farm down in the valley below on the left. Keep walking alongside the hedgerow to a metal stile in the fenceline ahead. Cross a stile and continue ahead to a white cottage. Skirt around the field edge in front of the cottage and walk across the drive to cross a delapidated stile, just beyond a barn, into the next field. Follow a narrow sheep track along the edge of the field, passing small rocky outcrops. Cross the next stile and follow the left-hand fenceline across this field to a stile onto the lane.

Turn left onto a lane and continue downhill for aprroximately 600m, passing Nant Bach farm on the right and Nant Uchaf on the left at the bottom of the hill.

2. Continue along the lane, little more than a track now, with a stream down on the left. At a track junction, bear right on a grassy path along the hillside, ignoring the left fork that leads down to a farm. Go through a gate and continue ahead on the track until you reach the farmyard of an old derelict farmhouse.

Go through the gate into the farmyard, then turn right immediately through a gate beside the house and walk along the side of the house. Turn left and walk behind farm buildings, through another gate. Continue ahead for approximately 50m beyond buildings and go through another gate into the field.

Walk across the field beside the hedge towards farm buildings visible ahead. Partway across the field cross through a gate to the right-hand side of the hedge and continue walking along this field edge, passing barns and a farmyard on the left. Continue along the field edge until it joins a farm drive, then walk up the drive as it bears right. Part way up the drive, turn left through a gate and walk across the next field to a farm ahead. Pass the farmhouse on the right and go through two gates onto the farm drive. After a few metres bear right and follow this for approximately 300m, down to the road.

3. Turn left and walk downhill on the road. Where the road bends left, take the track on the right, beside a small building, signed to 'Ty-newydd-foel'.

There are superb views of the Snowdonian mountains on the left as you walk along this path—Moel Siabod stands apart on the left, then the Snowdon group, the jagged Glyderau and the more rounded Carneddau. The foreground of gentle green hills, broken by thick hedgrows and stone walls snaking up and down the valleys, is a pleasing contrast to this rugged backdrop.

Keep following this clear track past a couple of houses on the right. Go through a gate and continue on the track until it meets a farm drive (Plas-bychan). Turn right along the drive and continue over a cattle grid, now walking on a surfaced lane. Pass a drive to farm buildings on the right and continue along the lane as it bears left down to the road passing small lakes on the left (approx 800m from the first farm to the road). Turn right and walk along the road all the way back to the village (over 2km).

The imposing cream building on the hillside to the left, before you reach the village, is Garthewin, which was the family seat of the Wynne family for over three centuries until it was finally sold in 1996.

Moel Unben

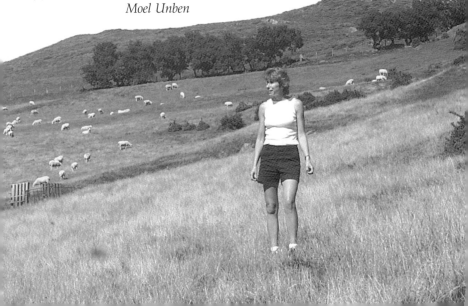

Cyffylliog

Distance: *8 km/5 miles*

A delightful walk from this unspoilt village that nestles amongst the tree clad hills of the Clwyedog valley. The walk leads along the upper reaches of the Clwyedog and then along quiet lanes with wide views out to sea. The return is made on an old track across farmland with views of the forested hills.

Start: *There is limited roadside parking in Cyffylliog. Grid ref: 060 578 (OS Explorer map 264).*

Cyffylliog has a peaceful air, hidden away in the valley bottom. The simple terraced cottages, the inn and village school, with its distinctive bell tower, are attractive, but it is the setting, high in the wooded Clywedog valley, threaded by narrow wildflower-edged lanes that gives its special quality.

The walk

1. This circuit is one of the waymarked walks in the Mynydd Hiraethog and Denbigh Moors footpath network developed by Conwy and Denbighshire Councils. It is waymarked with special 'Mynydd Hiraethog' green circular discs which will be seen throughout the walk.

At the staggered crossroads between the school and the Red Lion pub, take the lane uphill signed to "Nantglyn". Pass the church on the right.

Cyffylliog church is small with a simple stone bell tower, set in a pretty churchyard with old gnarled yews. Next to the churchyard is a Georgian 'Hearse house', a small stone building with large wooden doors, built to house the horse-drawn hearse.

Just past the church, take the waymarked footpath on the right. Pass a cottage on the left and continue into woodland. Cross a footbridge over the river and follow the path to the left, walking with the river on your left.

Before stepping stones across the river, turn right along the waymarked path keeping the river on the left. Follow this path through woodland for approximately 1km as it climbs gradually up the hillside, with the river below on the left.

The Clywedog is fast flowing here running over large slabs of stone and forming small waterfalls. An attractive mix of trees including wild cherry and hazel grow on the steep banks which are carpeted with wild garlic in spring.

Ignore a path on the right and continue ahead on a lower path through a gate. Continue ahead through a second gate and keep on the grassy waymarked path, passing a pond down on the left and a cottage on the right. Go through a gateway beyond the cottage, then bear right immediately (before the river) on a path that leads along the righthand side of the river, ignoring the small bridge and wider track ahead. The path widens as it climbs up the hillside, with conifers on the right and a steep drop down to the river on the left. Continue on the path as it bears right away from the river. At the first path junction bear left, following the waymarker. At the path T junction turn right and continue uphill for approximately 750m.

2. Cross a gate or stile at the edge of the forestry plantation into more open grassland. A few paces beyond the gate turn left and cross a stile in the fenceline. Contour across a large field above the river. Bear left at the waymarker post to a stile in the far left-hand corner of the field. Cross the stile and walk beside a fence along a narrow path with the river down on the left. Cross another stile and follow the fenceline—the path isn't very clear in places, but keep going straight ahead keeping the river on the left. Cross another stile and continue along the riverside path to a road.

Turn right along the road which climbs steeply uphill to a T junction. Turn right and continue along the road for about 2km.

There are wide views to the left stretching out to sea. In the foreground is the green rolling farmland of the Vale of Clwyd with the tower of Llanrhaeadr church just visible on a clear day and the northern Clywdians beyond. As you walk along the lane, views of the Clwydians change, as first Moel Arthur and then Moel Famau appear.

3. At a fork in the road, bear right, passing stone buildings on the left and another track. Ignore a footpath signed right and continue ahead for 100m over a cattle grid, then take a clearly waymarked footpath immediately on the left. Follow this very

Beside Afon Clywedog, Cyffylliog

clear grassy track for approximately 1½ km, gradually descending towards Cyffylliog.

The views are superb again with the Clocaenog Forest across the valley and rolling farmland with thick hedges and pockets of woodland all around.

At a gate and stile, cross over and continue ahead to the road. Turn right and walk along the road downhill. Pass a left-hand turn continuing ahead downhill. At the bottom of the hill turn right, cross the river on the main bridge and walk back into the village, passing the village school on the left.

Clocaenog Forest

Distance: *9½ km/6 miles*

A refreshing walk through the hilly coniferous forest and along quiet lanes with some superb views.

NB - Please note that this is a working forest and felling operations may occasionally affect some of the paths.

Start: *There is a small pull-in and limited roadside parking around the signed footpath to Pincyn Llys, 2 miles west of Bontuchel. Grid ref: 065 557 (OS Explorer map 264).*

The walk

1. From the pull-in take the path signed to "Pincyn Llys" leading uphill through fairly open woodland with bilberry and heather. (Path is also marked with pink Mynydd Hiraethog waymarkers as some of this route overlaps with sections of the Mynydd Hiraethog linear footpath.) Cross a forest track and continue straight ahead on the waymarked path uphill towards a clearing. Follow the path to the large stone obelisk at the top of the hill.

This is the Lord Bagot Monument. The Bagots were important landowners in the area whose estate extended over 17,500 acres in the 18th and 19th centuries. The monument was erected by the second Lord Bagot in 1832 to commemorate the planting of the surrounding conifer plantations. They were felled during the First World War and the present forest was established in 1930s when the Forestry Commission began to replant the area.

There are fine panoramic views from the monument—the Arans beyond Bala can be seen to the southwest; the Berwyns to the southeast and the Clwydians to the east with the rolling Vale of Clwyd in the foreground and the lower wooded hills around Bontuchel to the north.

From the monument, facing back down the original path, walk forward a few metres, then turn left and follow a narrow grassy path, running west into the trees. Keep on this path through the plantations. Keep going in same direction until you reach a junction where two wide forestry tracks merge. Continue ahead on the forestry track for ¾km until it meets the road.

Turn left and walk along the road for just over 1km, ignoring the first forestry track on the left.

2. Soon after "Cefn Ddu" cottage on the right, turn left along an unwaymarked broad forestry track. Follow this track passing an overgrown lake on the right (ignore a track on the left opposite the lake).

Look for the white fluffy flower heads of bog cotton in the summer and the colourful dragonflies that breed in the acidic water. The dark green rushes and yellow and red sphagnum mosses indicate the boggy areas around the open water.

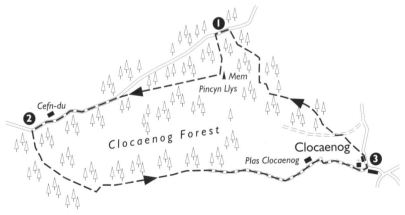

Where the path joins from the right, beside a fingerpost, continue ahead, once again on the "Mynydd Hiraethog" waymarked route. At the next path junction take the waymarked track on the left. At a T junction in front of a gate into fields, turn left and then bear right, following the waymarker. Continue on this path which skirts the edge of the forest with farmland on the right.

At the next path junction beside a finger post, leave the main forestry track which curves left, and continue ahead on a smaller path leading downhill. At the next path junction, take the right-hand path that gradually leads away from the forest and has wide open views. Continue along this path as it descends to join a lane. Continue downhill on the lane, passing the attractive but disused Plas Clocaenog farm on the right. Follow the lane to the village of Clocaenog.

The pretty church at Clocaenog, with its simple bellcote, stands on a hillock above the village. Its position may have given the village its name as 'Clocaenog' means 'grassy knoll'.

3. Pass the church and turn left at the road junction. At the edge of the village, cross a stile on the left and walk diagonally through the centre of the field to another stile in the bottom fenceline. Cross a boggy area beyond the stile, then over a small footbridge and climb steeply up the field to another stile. Cross onto a track and turn left. Walk along the track a few metres and then take a narrow path on the right along the woodland edge. The path climbs steeply uphill with fields on the right and woods on the left. Cross a forestry track and continue ahead on a narrow path, still climbing.

At the top of the hill continue ahead where the path joins a broader forestry track and the land is more open (ignore track off to left).

There are now wide views of the Clwydian Range on the right.

Pass a small white cottage on the right, just before another spur of forest. At the first path junction, where a track leads

Field path on the edge of Clocaenog village

down to the cottage, bear left and at a T junction a little further on, take the track to the right (a more direct route is to follow the public footpath straight ahead, but it is not marked and may be overgrown and impassable in the summer). Follow the track for about 1km as it contours round the hillside through more woodland. At path intersections, continue ahead on the same track until it meets the road. (The final 250metres is not a right of way but public access is allowed.) Turn left and walk a few metres back to the pull-in by the Pincyn Llys sign.

Melin-y-Wig & Derwen

Distance: *12 km/8 miles*

A longer but varied walk through forest, a quiet lane that was once a pilgrims' route and attractive riverside.

NB - The section through the forest south of the car park is very boggy. Waterproof boots are essential and it is rough underfoot. If you prefer you can avoid that section by just doing the loop from Derwen to Melin-y-Wig. (see map).

Start: *Park at Boncyn Foel-Bach Forest Enterprise car park. There are picnic tables on the hillside here with wide views across the Vale of Clwyd.*

(There are more facilities—toilets, and a pleasant lakeside walk—at the larger Forest Enterprise car park at Bod Petryal 2km further along the road but the footpaths don't easily link with this route.) Grid ref: 055 520 (OS Explorer map 264).

The Route

1. From the car park climb steps past picnic tables and walk uphill keeping a fence on the left and felled trees on the right. At the corner of a field turn left onto a clear path along a beech avenue, with a laid beech hedge on one side.

Keep on the same path as it bears left and continue to the road. Cross road, turn right and walk along the road a few yards to a footpath sign. Turn left along the path passing farm buildings on the right (Glan-y-Gors). Beyond the buildings go through a gate and cross the field to a stile in the opposite fence. Cross the stile and continue on a narrow cleared path through a forested area. Cross a wide forest track and continue straight ahead up the bank and along a path through conifers. (NB - This section can be extremely boggy.) Climb a stile into fields and follow a sunken grassy path between old stone walls down the hillside.

The mound on the hillside to left is a Stone Age burial cairn. Lovely views open out here of the gorse capped, sheep grazed hills, dotted with twisted trees and with stone walls snaking up the hillsides. Buzzards are common, circling and crying overhead.

2. When you reach a farm drive, either continue straight ahead along the drive to join a lane or, if you prefer to reduce the road walking, turn right through a gate and follow the footpath to another farm on the right. Walk through the farmyard and along the farm drive to the lane. (NB - This section of path can be muddy and there may be horses and other stock in paddocks by the farm.)

This quiet winding lane formed part of the medieval pilgrim track from St Winifred's Well at Holywell in the north-east corner of Wales, to the tomb of St David in Pembrokeshire at its south-western most tip.

Turn right and walk along the lane for 3km finally walking downhill into Melin-y-Wig.

Milling was obviously important here as "Melin" means "mill". The old stone buildings on the right near the bridge over the river may once have been part of the mill complex.

3. At a road junction just beyond the bridge bear left and after a few metres turn left along a drive just beyond a chapel. Partway down the drive turn right over a stile and follow the path along the right-hand riverbank. Continue ahead when the path joins a grassy track leading in front of a cottage with the river on the left. Cross a footbridge over the river and turn right, following a narrow path along the left-hand bank of the river. Continue in the same direction, keeping the river on your right.

Climb a stile and follow the path across the base of a forested hillside with the river below on the right. (NB - At the time of writing felling and extraction was in progress.) Follow this path as it contours along the lower hillside near the river. Where the main forest path bears slightly left and starts to climb, continue ahead on a lower path along the riverside.

(NB - This riverside path was blocked by brashing and overgrown when route was originally walked but had been cleared when route was rechecked in October 2000. If the path becomes overgrown again follow the forest track uphill, then turn right at a track T junction onto a broader forestry track and follow this as it curves round the hillside and then descends into the next valley. At the bottom of the hill cross a stile to rejoin the riverside path.)

The wooded hill on the opposite side of the river is crowned by an Iron Age hillfort ("Dinas" on the OS maps) but it is difficult to pick out the ramparts nowadays due to the tree cover.

Follow the path along a fenceline as it bears left away from the river to a stile. Cross the stile and continue ahead across a grassy meadow beside the river. (NB - Can be wet!) Pass the stile from the forestry track on the left and continue ahead beside the river keeping the fence on the left. Continue ahead, crossing a log fence until you reach an old broken stile in the fence ahead. Cross this stile by the fence corner and go slightly left uphill for about 30m to meet a curving track. Turn right and follow the track back down to a meadow beside the river. Walk across the meadow (NB - Can be boggy!) and over a stile into the next field. Cross the field and go through a gate leading past an old cottage on the left. Continue along the drive of the cottage.

There are good views across the valley. The limestone quarry on the opposite hillside is one of several in the area, providing the mellow grey stone used in many of the local buildings.

After about 1km the drive bears left beside farm buildings (Glyn Mawr) and becomes a lane. Continue along the lane for about 1km, as it contours along the valley, passing another small cottage on the left and later a larger farm, until you reach Derwen.

You may wish to detour into the churchyard of the medieval church to see the fine 15th century preaching cross in the churchyard.

3. At the road junction opposite Derwen church, cross the road, then turn left and walk round the churchyard walls. Take the left turn at the end of a row of cottages opposite.

Derwen church and medieval preaching cross

Follow this lane to a small junction beside a chapel on the left. Take the tiny lane opposite which quickly deteriorates to become an overgrown track. Where the track narrows, after approximately 250m, go through a gate on the left and walk across a large field aiming for tall trees on the skyline ahead. Go through a gate in the fenceline to the left of trees and then walk down the right-hand edge of the next field to a road. If the stile in the hedge isn't visible at the bottom of the field, (impossible to find at the time of writing, although the path is signed from the road!) turn left and walk to a gate in the field corner and climb over onto the road. Turn right along the road and continue for 750m, passing 'Minffordd' cottage and Glan-y-aber farm track entrance, to the drive to Braich farm on the left.

Just before Braich Farm drive behind a stone wall and hedge on the left is *'Ffynnon Sarah'*, a medieval holy well.

Detour through the gate onto a paved flat path that leads to where the spring bubbles into a tree shaded stone bath, now green with moss. The water was believed to have cured rheumatism and cancer. Pilgrims dropped in gifts of pins and those cured left their sticks and crutches as thanks offerings. It was still in use in Victorian times.

Take the next track on the left up to Braich farm. Walk between a barn on the left and the farmhouse on the right, then turn through a small gate into the farm garden and straight ahead to a field gate. Walk up the next field parallel to a stream on the right-hand side to a gate in the top corner. Go through the gate and bear right on a muddy grassy track along the field edge climbing uphill. Go over the next stile and follow the grassy track diagonally up the field to a waymarker post and stile beside the road. Turn left onto the road and walk back to the forestry carpark.

Llangernyw

Distance: *6 km/3¾ miles*

A delightful walk centred upon the pretty village of Llangernyw, leading along a terraced woodland path beside a cascading stream through the former 'pleasure gardens' of Hafodunos Hall. The return to the village is along peaceful lanes and beside the Afon Elwy.

Start: Park near the public toilets (left down the lane beside the church) or the car park beside the Henry Jones Museum (opposite the Bridge Inn).

Grid ref: 876 674 (OS Outdoor Leisure map 17).

Llangernyw is a very pretty village with its whitewashed church and old inn, set amongst rolling hills. St Digain's church has been a Christian place of worship since the 6th century but the 4,000 year old yew—the oldest in Wales—may indicate that it was originally a pagan site of worship as Christian churches were often sited on earlier pagan sites for continuity of worship.

The walk

1. From the church turn left along the main road towards Llanrwst. Turn right beside the Bridge Inn and follow the path alongside the pub to the riverside. (Muddy at the time of writing due to works going on by the river). Go through a kissing gate and walk across the field, keeping close to the river, to a small footbridge. Cross the river and walk along the path to the road. Turn left along the road and, a few metres up the hill, turn left on a signed footpath, beside a delapidated gatehouse, along the old drive of Hafodunos Hall.

'Hafodunos'—'house of one night'—is a name more usually given to one of the tiny temporary homes of the herdsmen taking livestock up for summer grazing on the moors. At first one wonders how this name came to be given to such a grand house that obviously took years to complete. However, it was built on the site of a monastery and there may have been a rest house there for pilgrims—hence 'house of one night'.

About 60m along the drive turn left onto a waymarked footpath into woods. This section along the river is very clearly waymarked and well maintained with steps and handrails so the route directions are not detailed. Bear right down steps towards the river. Continue along this delightful path, eventually zigzagging uphill away from the river.

This section of the walk leads through what was once part of the pleasure gardens of the house and it is was planted luxuriantly with exotic species—the rhododendrons on the banks and clumps of bamboo nearer the river are the most obvious that remain. These blend well with the natural woodland that clothes the opposite bank, with the fast flowing river below, cutting through stone, with small waterfalls as it tumbles down the hillside. Damp loving plants like golden saxifrage, a small yellowish green plant with rounded leaves, ferns and mosses abound. Pale green feathery lichens hang down from the trees. They only grow in areas that are pollution free, so their abundance here indicates how clean the air is.

Follow the woodland path (still waymarked) to a ladder stile on the woodland edge. Cross the stile and continue ahead, through a small gate and continue ahead, skirting woodland on the right, with the river on the left. Cross a footbridge over the stream and walk up stone steps, then along the field edge. Climb another ladder stile and walk

The memorial to the Sandbach family

ahead, bearing slightly left across this large field to a hedge on the far side (follow direction of waymarker). Turn right at the field boundary and continue along the left-hand field edge to a gate in the far left corner. Beyond the gate, follow the path to the road.

2. Turn left along the road and, when you reach a junction with a grassy triangle in the centre, bear right along a narrow lane. Pass several buildings and continue along the lane which becomes more overgrown and track-like. When the track joins a road, turn right and, after 120m, turn left at the next junction, signed 'Gwytherin'.

Follow this lane past farm buildings and bear left at the first road junction. Continue to a T junction and turn left. Follow this quiet road to a bridge over the river. Turn left onto a footpath just before the bridge. Meander through the field and grassy clearing keeping the river on your right, then cross a stile concealed in the far left-hand corner of the field and climb uphill on an overgrown grassy path with the river down on the right. Cross two more stiles into a large field (ignore a waymarker to the left) and continue walking ahead beside the river. At the next field boundary, cross a stile and walk across the field, keeping the river on the right, to a small footbridge in the middle of the field. Cross the bridge, turn right and follow the left-hand hedgerow to a smaller footbridge. Continue to a stile onto the road by a stone bridge. Turn left along the road to return to the village, detouring through the churchyard on the left if preferred.

The large stone mausoleum stands out amongst the gravestones in the churchyard. It bears testament to the wealth and influence of the Sandbach family—Samuel Sandbach, a Liverpool merchant and shipowner, bought nearby Hafodunos Hall in 1831 and several generations of the family have left their mark on the village.

Llansannan

Distance: *12 km/8 miles*

A longer but varied walk alongside the River Aled and its tributaries, through rolling pasture edged with thick hedgerows and pockets of woodland, with a backdrop of mountains.

*This circuit follows sections of a series of waymarked walks developed by Conway County Borough Council. For further information on the complete booklet, '***Walks around Rural Conwy'***, contact the council on: 01492 575200.*

Start: *Park in the car park opposite the Post Office, behind the public toilets in Llansannan village.*
Grid ref: 933 658 (OS Explorer map 264).

The walk

1. From the car park turn right and walk to the road junction opposite the Red Lion. Turn left and walk along the road, past the Saracen's Head pub. Just after the road crosses the river, take the footpath signed on the left, opposite a white house 'Y Llety', along a clear track. Cross a cattle grid and continue along the track which gradually descends to the riverside.

The wide fast flowing river is edged with trees—particularly alder that thrive in the damp conditions. Look for dippers—small brown birds with white breasts that bob across the rocks—and grey wagtails—slender grey birds with long tails and yellow undersides. Both are commonly seen, feeding on insects, on the rocky rivers and streams in the area.

At a T junction of tracks, turn left over a bridge and continue along the track over another cattle grid, ignoring a path signed off to the left. Pass a house on the right and continue on the rising track. Further on ignore a track off to the left.

Just before a house (Dyffryn Aled), bear right off the drive into a field then curve left to walk along the left-hand field edge, passing the house on the left. Just beyond the house cross a stile on the left and continue ahead through 'ornamental' grounds to join a woodland track. Continue on the woodland track going straight ahead at a path junction. At the end of the woodland, continue on the track beside a pasture. Cross a stile and walk along a grassy path to cross a footbridge over the river (Afon Aled).

2. Follow the track to the road. Turn left and walk downhill to a crossroads. Turn right here, signed to 'Capel Horeb' and 'Tan-y-Fron'. Follow the lane for ½km, passing 'The Old Mill' and walking beside the stream.

(If you want a more strenuous walk and are equipped with a detailed map, you may wish to detour up a footpath on the left into woodland, soon after 'The Old Mill' on right. This leads up Mynydd Tryfan which has wide views from the top. There is a clear track back down from Arllwyd farm which can link back to the road at Tan Tryfan, grid ref: 966 655.)

Where the lane starts to climb steeply, turn right onto a lane signed 'no through road'. In about 250m, just before buildings, turn right down a farm drive (Heskin). Follow the drive uphill and, where the drive bends right to the farm, cross a stile on the left (straight ahead as you approach). Take the path straight ahead across the field (ignore the other signed on the right). Cross another stile and walk along the lower edge of the next field, passing a pond on the left, with the river below. Towards the end of the field, follow a waymarker down to the bottom left corner by the river. Climb a stile, cross the stream and another stile and climb up the opposite bank.

Walk along the edge of the field above the river, bearing right and heading for a gate halfway along the hedge ahead. Go through the gate and continue ahead across a large field—don't go down to a footbridge over river down on the left—towards farm buildings. (Take care—no waymarkers here!) Keep metal barns on the left and go through a gate beside them into the farmyard. Follow the drive as it curves right past the farmhouse and outbuildings. Ignore a fork to the right, and continue along the drive to the road. Turn left along the road which climbs steeply for approximately 1km.

There are good views of Mynydd Tryfan on the left from this lane.

Where the gradient levels out, turn right on the lane signed

Beside Afon Aled

to 'Tan-y-Fron' and follow it for approximately 1½ km into the hamlet of Tan-y-fron.

There are glimpses of the Snowdonian mountains to the left.

3. Follow the lane over the bridge in Tan-y-fron past a simple chapel on the right with a house attached. About 60m uphill, take a footpath on left (the stile may be difficult to see in the hedgerow). Cross the field and climb another stile into the next field. Walk diagonally-right across the field, heading for tall clump of trees by the fence. (When bracken is high it may be easier to walk along the fence to the right of the stile and cross the field above the bracken line.)

Cross a stile and walk diagonally-right across the next field towards farm buildings. Go through a gate and turn left into the farmyard. Walk through the farmyard, passing the farmhouse on the right and walk along the farm drive to the road. (Alternatively, partway along the drive, take a signed path through fields on the right to cut the corner off).Turn right at the road and walk to a T junction with more major road. Cross this road and climb up the bank opposite and cross a stile near a modern bungalow. Cross two more stiles linking small enclosures, then continue ahead, keeping the fence on the left. After passing a large pond on the left cross through the next gateway, then turn right and continue in the same direction as before with the fence now on the right.

Buzzards wheel overhead and you may hear their high pitched 'mewing' cry. Rabbits scurry for the safety of the undergrowth—startled by your approach but also rushing to avoid the buzzard, whose favourite food is rabbit!

At the end of the field, join a wider track and continue ahead through a gate. Walk along the left-hand edge of a large field. Where the field widens, continue ahead, bearing slightly right, to a stile in the far corner.

Cross into a scrub edged field and walk across keeping near the fence on the right. At a dense patch of gorse, with a house visible on the right, pick your way down the bank on a narrow path through a gorse thicket to join the road. (If this public footpath is too overgrown, walk along the edge of the thicket downhill to a gate onto the road).

Turn left along the road and walk downhill. At a road junction, cross over and continue ahead on a little lane passing a stone cottage on the right. Continue on the path down to the river (Afon Aled). Ignore the bridge on the left and continue ahead on a small path along the right-hand bank of the river, passing an old mill on the left bank.

The Llansannan monument

The river is fast flowing here, tumbling over rocks and making a small waterfall. The mill wheel is no longer in place but it is easy to see why it was such a good location for the mill—harnessing the torrent of water here must have generated lots of power.

Follow the path along the river to the road. Cross the road and take the path immediately opposite, beside the river. Follow the left-hand fenceline of the field, with the river to the left. In the second small field bear right to a stile in the fence and a small footbridge. Cross the bridge, then turn left up the bank a little and walk beside the river along a faint grassy path that meanders through natural woodland. The path isn't always clear and crosses an area of bracken which will be tall in the summer but keep parallel to the river and to the right of fallen trees.

Where the path reaches a hedgerow cross a stile on the left just above the river and walk along the field edge, keeping the river on the left. Continue across fields in the same direction beside the river to a footbridge. Cross the footbridge, and then walk straight across the field to an old stone wall and hedge opposite. Turn right and walk along the track towards farm buildings. Go through a gate into the farmyard and follow the farm drive to the road. Turn right and follow the road back into Llansannan. At a T junction in the middle of the village turn right past a shop and then left before the Saracen's Head to return to the car park.

The statue on the left beside the road junction in the village centre is the Llansannan Monument—a girl in a Welsh dress in front of an obelisk. It was erected in 1899 to commemorate five writers born in the area over the preceding centuries.

Gwytherin

Distance: *6 km/3¾ miles*

A short but refreshing walk centred on this pretty and peaceful village, up a wooded valley and across open moorland with wide views of the Snowdonian mountains.

*This circuit follows sections of a series of waymarked walks developed by Conwy County Borough Council. For further information on the complete booklet, '**Walks around Rural Conwy**', contact the council on: **01492 575200**.*

NB - Some sections of this walk, across heather moorland, are extremely boggy. When visibility is poor, route finding across the moors may be a problem unless you have a map and compass, so save this walk for a dry clear day when the views of Snowdonia are spectacular and the moorland is alive with birdsong.

Start: *There is roadside parking in the village or large pub car park (ask the landlord's permission first).*
Grid ref: 877 615 (OS Outdoor Leisure map 17).

Gwytherin village centre is clustered around a small stone enclosed square containing an old anvil, edged by its simple church, pretty cottages and the Lion Inn. Legend has it that St Winifred, the martyred saint of Holywell, became an abbess of a convent here which is why Gwytherin church takes her name. In the attractive oval churchyard are four large stones that may date from the 5th century.

The walk

1. Opposite the church, take the footpath that runs alongside a stream to the right of the pub. Pass a cottage on the left and walk uphill along a narrow path, keeping the stream down on the left. Cross a stile and follow the waymarked path uphill. Gradually bear right away from woodland and the stream across the field (NB - the path isn't very clear) and find a stile and waymarker in the fence on the right. Cross the stile then turn right and walk towards low stone buildings and sheep pens—this is the sheep dipping area of Pen-y-graig farm so please take care. Continue ahead, keeping buildings on the right, then turn right, cross a stile and turn left onto a track leading uphill away from the buildings.

Keep walking on this clear track, for about 800m, going through one gateway and ignoring the first path on the right by another gate. When you reach a fence ahead and the main path bears right through a gate, turn left and walk across moorland, keeping the fence on the right. Turn left and walk across moorland, keeping the fence on the right.

Looking northwest from Ffrithuchaf

During the spring and summer the moor is filled with the haunting call of the curlew—a high pitched 'coorl-li' and you are likely to see some of these large waders with their long down-curved beaks as they take off at your approach. They spend winter on the coast and then fly inland to breed on the moors.

Heather thrives in the drier areas—the delicate pale lilac flowered ling and bell heather with its larger bright pinkish-purple flowers. In the many wetter areas are dark green rushes, red tinged grasses and patches of green and red moss—much of it is sphagnum, the spongy moss that horticulturalists use to line their hanging baskets as it holds water so well.

Follow this fenceline across the moor. (NB - this section can be extremely boggy.) At a T junction of fences turn left and keep walking with the fence on your right. Ignore a stile and waymarker on the right soon after this (If it is very misty you may prefer to follow this waymarked path across fields to the road, then turn right and right again along the road back to Gwytherin, rather than continue across the open moorland.) and continue walking along the fenceline.

Go through a gate and keep walking straight ahead, keeping the fence on the right until you reach a stile at the fence junction ahead. Cross a stile and bear diagonally-left downhill across a hummocky boggy grassy field. Cross a ditch running down the field and walk downhill parallel to the fence on the left and a ditch on the right to a fence ahead. Go through a gate in the corner of the field ahead (the path is waymarked over a stile to the right of a gate but it's extremely boggy!) and walk downhill across the field to a gate onto the road.

There are wide views of the Snowdonian peaks ahead on a clear day. Moel Siabod is the bulky peak to the left followed by the Snowdon group, the Glyderau, Tryfan and rounded bulk of the Carneddau.

Turn left and walk down the road. Turn left at a T junction and continue walking downhill back into the village.

Stones in Gwytherin churchyard

Llyn Brenig

Distance: *12 km/8 miles or 5 km/3 miles*

Enjoy the open water of Llyn Brenig, fringed with conifer forests and the wild Hiraethog moors.

Start: *Pay and display parking is available at Llyn Brenig Visitor Centre.*

Grid ref: 967 548 (OS Explorer map 264).

Welsh Water, who manage the reservoirs, encourage visitors and have developed a variety of walks:- a surfaced, easy to follow 10½ mile circular walk around the lake; a 2 mile archaelogical trail from the car park on the eastern side; and a 1¼ mile nature trail on the north western side. A good starting point for a first visit is the visitor centre where the trail leaflets can be bought and there are informative displays. There is also an adventure playground and cafe so it makes an ideal family outing.

If you want a more varied walk, the one described here links a walk along the dam wall with a pleasant exploration of the Aled valley beyond the dam. The circuit around Pentre-llyn-cymmer is one of a series of walks in the Mynydd Hiraethog and Denbigh Moors footpath network developed by Conwy and Denbighshire Councils. It is waymarked with distinctive 'Mynydd Hiraethog' green circular discs.

If you just want a very short circuit including the dam a shorter but less interesting option is also described.

The walk

1. Park in the main Visitor Centre car park. Walk down to the reservoir edge past the Visitor Centre and turn right along the water's edge. Go through a small gate and follow this path alongside the reservoir to the dam. Turn left and walk along the wide track which tops the dam wall.

The high rainfall and low population on the moors made it an ideal site for a reservoir. The first scheme was proposed in the 1900s to provide water for Birkenhead. Construction of the Alwen reservoir was completed in 1916 but it was not until 1976 that Lyn Brenig was opened. The reservoirs now provide water for industrial and domestic use in Chester and northeast Wales and are used to regulate the flow of water in the River Dee, preventing flooding in the winter and drought in the summer. The small tower in the water beside the dam regulates the flow of water from the reservoir.

There are wide views from the dam across the moors and forested hilltops. 3,500 years ago Bronze Age tribesmen hunted on these moors and the area is dotted with their burial mounds. Many have been carefully excavated and several

well preserved examples can be seen on the archaelogical trail to the northeast.

At the end of the dam take the track on the right that curves down behind the dam. After about 80m, turn left along a grassy track leading above a stream and weir in the valley below on the right. Cross a stile into the forest and, after a few metres, turn right and walk along a path at edge of trees. At the woodland edge go through a gate onto a lane. Continue on this lane over a bridge and uphill.

(If you want a short route, turn right onto a signed footpath partway up the lane. Walk diagonally-right across the field and strip of woodland to the road. Turn right onto a narrow road and follow this back below the dam to the lefthand (western) side of reservoir.)

Follow the lane to a road junction. Continue ahead along the road, bearing sharply left and downhill after 150m. Continue past farm buildings on the right to a T junction at the bottom of the hill. Turn right and walk along the road into the hamlet of Pentre-llyn-cymmer.

2. Turn left across a small bridge towards the Outdoor Pursuits Centre and right along a track in front of this. Climb a stile by a gate, then left over a second stile and take a path on the left, skirting along the left-hand edge of a large field. (The route is waymarked from now on with the Mynydd Hiraethog green discs—the other path marked straight ahead is the return route.)

At the end of the field cross a stile and continue ahead across the next field, with the river below on the left. Continue across fields, gradually descending to walk alongside the river. Pass a cottage on the opposite bank and walk towards woodland ahead.

The river edge is full of colour in summer—pinkish-white valerian, cream meadowsweet, masses of buttercups, tall pale green reeds and darker green rushes.

Climb a stile into woodland and follow a meandering narrow path through damp ground alongside the river. At the end of the woodland turn right away from the river skirting around the right-hand side of a hill ahead.

This small hill, Caer Ddunod, was once fortified and, although ruined by 17th century, may have once been of considerable importance—some even claim it was the site of Caractacus' last stand against the Romans!

Cross a stile and gate and follow a track into a farmyard. Turn right past the farmhouse and continue along the farm drive. Where the drive meets a lane turn right and walk downhill, past a whitewashed cottage on the left. Where the main lane bends left, turn right onto a side lane and continue on this lane for over 1km, climbing quite steeply uphill.

The dam, Llyn Brenig

3. After the lane bends sharply right, the angle eases. At the next sharp left-hand bend, with a farm, "Hafoty Llechwedd", on the right, take the signed path straight ahead, leading behind the buildings.

A 'hafoty' or 'hafod' was a small summer dwelling, built by the herdsmen who brought cattle to graze the moors in the summer. There were many of these simple one-roomed stone huts in the 16th and 17th centuries but they fell into disuse as sheep farming gradually took over—as sheep do not require milking, the shepherds didn't need to live with the flocks. Perhaps one of the older farm buildings here may have originally been a 'hafoty'?

Go through the gate or stile and walk along the top of the next field. Go through a gateway then turn left over a stile and walk diagonally-left across a large field, heading towards the left-hand edge of conifers. Pass a 'pile of stones' in the middle of the field.

There are good views to the left of the Alwyn Reservoir. The dam is particularly attractive with its turreted, romantic-looking water tower—quite different from the utilitarian one built at Brenig in the 1970s, but serving the same purpose.

Cross the stile and walk along the right-hand edge of the next field, beside trees. Go through a gate at end of the woodland and walk a short distance ahead along a wide track. Leave the main track, just after another track joins from the right, and walk diagonally-right across rough grass to a stile in the bottom right corner of the field. (Take care as, at time of writing, this wasn't waymarked and could easily be overlooked.)

Continue downhill along the right-hand fenceline to cross a stile on the right and continue downhill along the left-hand fenceline, following waymarker, back down to the path in front of the Outdoor Pursuits Centre. Retrace your steps turning right along the lane and left up the lane past the farm.

Continue uphill and soon after the lane bears sharply right, bear left instead of turning right onto the narrow lane that you used earlier. Follow this road back to the dam and either turn right to climb back onto the dam or left and follow the road below the dam back to the left-hand (western) side of the reservoir. Retrace your steps along reservoir edge back to the Visitor Centre.

Mara Books - www.marabooks.co.uk

Mara Books publish a range of walking and local interest books for Cheshire and North Wales and have the following list to date.

North Wales

Coastal Walks around Anglesey (volume 1)
ISBN 0 9522409 6 3. A collection of 15 walks which explore the varied scenery of Anglesey's beautiful coastline.

Coastal Walks around Anglesey Volume 2
ISBN 0 9522409 5 5. A companion volume to the above book, outlining 15 new walks spread around Anglesey's fascinating and beautiful coastline.

Circular Walks in the Conwy Valley
ISBN 0 9522409 7 1. A collection of circular walks which explore the varied scenery of this beautiful valley from the Great Orme to Betws-y-Coed.

Walking on the Lleyn Peninsula
ISBN 1 902512 00 6. A collection of circular walks which explore the wild and beautiful coastline and hills of the Lleyn Peninsula.

Walking in the Clwydian Hills and the Vale of Llangollen
ISBN 0 9522409 3 9. A collection of circular walks exploring the beautiful hills and valleys of the Welsh borders.

Circular walks along the Offa's Dyke Path
Volume 1 Prestatyn to Welshpool ISBN 1 902512 01 4.
Volume 2 Welshpool to Hay-on-Wye ISBN 1 902512 07 3.
The first volumes in a series which will sample some of the finest sections of this popular National Trail.

Walking in Snowdonia Volume 1—the northern valleys
ISBN 1 902512 06 5. 20 circular walks in the valleys amd lower hillsides of northern Snowdonia.

Cheshire

A Walker's Guide to the Wirral Shore Way

ISBN 0 9522409 0 4. This book describes a linear walk of 23 miles following Wirral's old coastline between Chester and Hoylake.

Circular Walks along the Sandstone Trail

ISBN 0 9522409 2 0. The Sandstone Trail is Cheshire's best known and most popular walking route. This book gives a complete route description along with 12 circular walks covering the entire trail.

Circular Walks along the Gritstone Trail
and Mow Cop Trail

ISBN 0 9522409 4 7. A route which follows Cheshire's eastern border along the edge of the Peak District. Following the same format as the Sandstone Trail book—a full description for both trails is combined with 12 circular walks.

Circular Walks in Wirral

ISBN 1 902512 02 2. A collection of circular walks in the coast and countryside of Wirral.

Local History

Picturesque Wirral

ISBN 0 9522409 9 8. A reprint of part of T A Coward's "Picturesque Cheshire" dealing with Wirral, originally published in 1903. A fascinating glimpse of Wirral in the closing years of the nineteenth century.

Picturesque Cheshire—Chester and the Welsh border

ISBN 1 902512 03 0. Like the above, this is a reprint of two chapters from T A Coward's "Picturesque Cheshire", originally published in 1903, dealing with the city of Chester and the western limits of the county bordering Wales. A fascinating glimpse of this historic city in the closing years of the nineteenth century.

119